teachers, tangibles, techniques:

COMPREHENSION OF CONTENT IN READING

Bonnie Smith Schulwitz, *Editor*
Central Michigan University

INTERNATIONAL READING ASSOCIATION
800 Barksdale Road   Newark, Delaware 19711

INTERNATIONAL READING ASSOCIATION

Copyright 1975 by the
International Reading Association, Inc.
Library of Congress Cataloging in Publication Data

Main entry under title:
Teachers, tangibles, techniques.

   Compilation of papers from IRA's Denver and Atlantic City conventions.
   Includes bibliographies.
     1. Reading—Addresses, essays, lectures.
2. Language arts—Addresses, essays, lectures.
I. Schulwitz,Bonnie Smith.   II. International Reading Association.
LB1050.T35   428'.4'071   75-5840
ISBN 0-87207-472-2

Second printing, October 1977

contents

COMPREHENSION OF CONTENT IN READING

TEACHERS

TANGIBLES

TECHNIQUES

foreword

Reading comprehension is a world problem because for centuries teachers around the world assumed that comprehension would be a natural consequence of decoding alone. In fact, the word *comprehension* itself is still to be invented in some of the languages of the world. In a few countries the word *comprehension* and the expression *reading comprehension* have been used by educators for some time, but readers in those countries still do not comprehend what they read so well as they should.

Early in the present century, scholars classified the kinds of comprehension involved in reading printed material and developed questions which teachers could ask to set the reader toward the goal —the right answer. Why didn't it work? Much material is now available to give the reader exercise in different kinds of comprehension. Why, with all of that, are readers still deficient? Between asking questions and getting answers there must be a kind of teaching (as well as a kind of wisdom about children, reading, and materials) which does not usually take place.

In ideographic languages, such as Chinese, children have been taught the meaning of each ideograph. In phonetic writing systems, such as English, in which the letter *a*, for example, represents different sounds in accordance with its environment, teachers have taken great pains to explain the consequences of these varied relationships and to have children discover and practice them for themselves. A very small modification of an ideograph, likewise, alters the meaning, and children must learn to observe these slight differences in form as indicative of possibly great differences in meaning. Comparable assistance in discovering word, phrase, sentence, and larger-unit relationships has been slow to develop because the basis for it has been little understood.

Now, through theory and research in a number of disciplines, it is obvious that different backgrounds brought to reading make many answers right; that children's uneven grasp of concepts, of language-embedded cognitive signals, and of linguistic patterns supportive of them must be a major concern of the good teacher and the good producer of materials. Furthermore, the teacher must add to his excellence in analysis of what the material demands, excellence in understanding the task of reading from the reader's point of view.

The International Reading Association is fortunate in the services of Bonnie Smith Schulwitz as editor of this compilation of papers from the Denver and Atlantic City Conventions, and in the generosity of the authors of those papers, so that teachers and publishers everywhere can derive implications for their work toward a more productive literacy for every reader. As for me, I'm glad I lived so long.

Constance M. McCullough, *President*
International Reading Association
1974-1975

introduction

The ardent search for means to build better readers seems always to be a journey, never a destination. Yet, the creative minds of teachers and researchers continually bring renewed insights to aid us on this journey. Each year the International Reading Association's annual convention provides a forum for the exchange of insights. So that teachers who are working directly with elementary and secondary students in our schools may profit from the convention forum, the Association publishes volumes of selected convention papers. Through this means, hopefully, more of us involved in helping children can increase our knowledge and repertoire of teaching techniques.

The papers included in this volume were selected for their perceptive insights and for their practical applicability to classroom teaching. It is hoped that the ideas presented will help elementary and secondary teachers to produce better readers at all grade levels and in all subject areas.

Most of the articles in *Teachers, Tangibles, Techniques: Comprehension of Content in Reading* were originally presented at IRA's 1973 Denver Convention organized by President William K. Durr around the theme "Reading—Power to the Pupil." This aptly chosen theme provides us with a significant purpose for reading this volume. If we are successful in developing greater reading power in our students, we will accomplish one of our most worthy goals as teachers.

Authors of this volume concentrate on views about developing more competent readers in the content areas, although the ideas contribute significantly to the knowledge of any teacher. While treatment of the subject is not exhaustively comprehensive, depth and scope of exploration are provided.

The divisions within this volume focus attention on four major areas. The first part, "Comprehension of Content in Reading," provokes thought about some critical factors affecting reading comprehension. Thus, some basic considerations structure a perspective for deeper exploration of comprehension in content reading.

Part two, "Teachers," reminds us of the ever present human facet of reading instruction. Despite the development of valuable teaching tangibles (resources and materials) and creative techniques, the vital teacher factor can never be ignored. Those involved in preservice and inservice teacher education programs may find these ideas especially useful.

Effective teachers utilize the available tangibles within the educational environment to help pupils develop competency in reading skills. Some suggestions for materials are enumerated in the section on "Tangibles."

Finally, effective teachers, equipped with tangibles, incorporate innovative techniques to build better readers. The final section, "Techniques," discusses some productive methods.

The formula evolves. Effective teachers who utilize valuable tangibles and apply innovative techniques have greater opportunity to bring each pupil closer to the goal of competency in reading. What better formula for delivering greater reading power to the pupil!

BSS

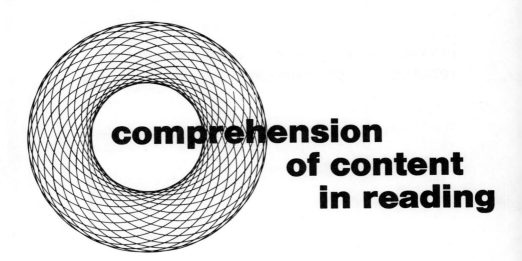

**comprehension
of content
in reading**

This paper compares and classifies models of comprehension and serves as a good introduction to this section on reading comprehension.

classroom implications from models of reading comprehension

w. john harker
university of victoria

The ultimate objective for teaching reading is to ensure that pupils understand what they read. The extent of a pupil's success in reading is determined by the degree to which he understands the meaning intended by the writer. This understanding is usually referred to as comprehension.

In spite of its importance, comprehension remains one of the least understood aspects of reading. Currently, the teaching of comprehension is almost exclusively based on the S-R paradigm. Skills are defined, taught, and measured; yet, the covert learning process involved in developing comprehension receives little attention. This situation is partly due to the fact that research and nonresearch investigations of comprehension are inconsistent and highly equivocal in their conclusions. One is forced to agree with Jenkinson (14) who has recently commented that "our ignorance of reading comprehension is pervasive and abysmal."

A relatively new approach to understanding comprehension has been the development of models of comprehension (10, 20). Beginning with Holmes' substrata factor model (12), recent years have witnessed the appearance of an increasing number of models of comprehension. While the avowed intention of many model builders has been to facilitate research into the nature of comprehension (9),

2   *Models of Reading Comprehension*

one would hope that these models could also suggest effective methods for teaching comprehension. The purpose of this discussion is to identify and to describe current models of comprehension in order to draw some conclusions regarding their application to classroom teaching.

categories of models

An immediate problem in developing an overview of comprehension models is that model builders differ in their conceptualizations of comprehension. Some models conceive comprehension in terms of the behaviors to be taught and the educational outcomes to serve as the foci of instruction (*1, 7, 17*). Other models are concerned with explaining cognitive operations associated with comprehension (*4, 23*). Still others approach comprehension by relating skills to cognitive operations (*21, 22*), while others describe comprehension in terms of information processing (*3, 13, 15, 16, 19*). A recent approach has been through psycholinguistic models (*2, 6, 17, 23*). In this discussion, models will be categorized according to the different approaches to comprehension which they demonstrate in order to assess the utility of each approach for classroom instruction.

behavioral models

The models of Gray and Robinson (*7, 17*) and Barrett (*1*) fall within this category. These models are primarily concerned with determining behavioral outcomes for teaching comprehension. In considering comprehension as one of the major aspects of reading, Gray and Robinson include three components of comprehension: *grasping literal meaning, securing an expanded grasp of the meaning*, and *understanding ideas read.* Similarly, Barrett includes *literal comprehension, inferential comprehension, evaluation*, and *appreciation* within his model. In addition, both models outline specific skills which they claim are exercised by comprehending readers. However, neither model is concerned with the cognitive operations which presumably underlie the performance of these skills. Robinson emphasizes this point when she states that the intent of her model is "to distinguish between *what* we are trying to achieve and the *processes* for achieving our goals." She is careful to note that "models of the reading process and of procedures for teaching reading have been omitted."

cognitive-based models

In contrast with the behavioral emphasis of the Gray-Robinson and the Barrett models, the models of Cleland (*4*) and Stauffer (*23*) are exclusively concerned with explaining cognitive operations underlying comprehension. Cleland defines comprehension as "a central mental activity involving the higher intellectual processes." He describes these processes as *perception, apperception, abstraction, appraisal, ideation,* and *application.* Similarly, Stauffer states that "reading is a complex phenomenon of mental activity akin to thinking," and that "to read is to comprehend what is read." He maintains that comprehension results from a cognitive process which involves *declaring purposes, reasoning while reading,* and *judging.* These models do not indicate what overt behaviors may be taken as evidence of the successful execution of the cognitive operations.

relational models

The models of Smith (*21*) and Spache (*22*) seek to explain comprehension by relating specific skills to postulated underlying cognitive operations. Both models adopt the *semantic content* dimension of Guilford's structure (*8*) of intellect model for this purpose. While Smith deletes some components from the Guilford model (claiming that they are not all directly applicable to comprehension), both models propose relationships between Guilford's cognitive operations and specific skills by which these operations are "exemplified in various reading behaviors" (*22*).

information-processing models

A wide variety of models is included in this category. Despite this variety, these models are alike in that they all attempt to explain comprehension in terms of the dynamic interaction between incoming information and the cognitive processing of this information.

Carver (*3*) conceives "the written verbal material which the human processes during reading" to be analogous to the information input of a computer. McCullough (*16*) views incoming verbal information in terms of a "schema of thought patterns" active in the mind of the writer and transmitted to the mind of the reader during reading. Similarly, Kingston (*15*) maintains that comprehension can best be understood "as a product of communication that results from interaction between the reader and the writer." Rystrom (*19*) explains the first stage of comprehension as the inputting of information which is decoded in the brain of the reader. Holmes and Singer (*13*) hypothesize that the information input during reading can be described as "coded audio-visual and kinesthetic impressions derived from the description of concrete objects."

The processing of this information is described by Carver in terms of computer data manipulation and storage resulting in "the understanding of the thoughts that the writer intended to communicate." Comprehension takes place in McCullough's model as a result of the reader's mind moving freely through a schema of thought patterns while employing inductive, deductive, convergent, divergent, and evaluative thinking. Kingston's model represents comprehension as resulting from the favorable influence of linguistic factors, reading skills, and psychological factors. Rystrom conceives information processing to involve vocabulary, syntax, item recall, item sequence, and evaluation. In the Holmes and Singer model, comprehension derives from the processing of information within a working system which Holmes (*13*) describes as follows:

> . . . as a result of the heightened cerebral activity engendered by increased concentration, conceptual abstractions are wrought by the process of comparing and contrasting the incoming information with relevant information already stored from past experiences. . . .

In all of these models, comprehension is conceived to be an entirely covert process having, in Carver's words, "no explicit output step." The behaviorist approach is therefore rejected as being an artificial representation of comprehension.

psycholinguistic models

Psycholinguistic models are characterized by the combination of psychological and linguistic theory in an attempt to explain comprehension. One feature of the psycholinguistic models is their linking of perception with cognition during the process of comprehension. Goodman (*5*) maintains that comprehension results from "a series of tentative decisions made on the basis of partial use of available language cues." As the reader progresses through a reading passage, he selects the correct meaning from various possible alternative meanings. This selection process is accomplished by means of visual scanning involving the use of different semantic and syntactic cues.

Hence, Goodman (6) describes comprehension as ''a psycholinguistic guessing game'':

> It involves partial use of available minimal language cues selected from perceptual input on the basis of the reader's expectation. As this partial information is processed, tentative decisions are made to be confirmed, rejected, or refined as reading progresses.

The models of Venezky and Calfee (24) and Brown (2) describe comprehension in a manner generally similar to Goodman. Ruddell (18) also describes comprehension through a psycholinguistic model. In remaining exclusively concerned with language processing, however, Ruddell does not account for visual scanning. He describes reading as:

> . . . a complex psycholinguistic behavior which consists of decoding written language units, processing the resulting language counterparts through structural and semantic dimensions, and interpreting the deep structure data relative to an individual's established objectives.

implications for teaching

No model of comprehension is specifically concerned with methods for teaching comprehension nor does any model present a developmental scheme describing how pupils learn to comprehend. The Gray-Robinson and the Barrett models are concerned with delineating desired outcomes for teaching comprehension, and the skills listed by Smith and Spache are intended to serve as objectives for instruction. But none of these models describes methods for realizing these objectives. Cognitive-based, information-processing, and psycholinguistic models all focus on the cognitive processes which presumably underlie comprehension. By adding linguistic considerations, psycholinguistic models compound the complexity of the cognitive process they describe without suggesting ways by which this process can be taught.

Despite these restrictions, models of comprehension do contain implications for teaching. The basic implication is that the traditional notion of teaching comprehension as a series of skills separately defined, sequentially developed, and generally applicable in any and all reading situations is in error. Models of comprehension clearly suggest that comprehension is a multidimensional process involving the cognitive processing of language. The performance of skills is merely the outer manifestation of this extremely complex inner process. The manner in which skills are applied to various comprehension tasks in different learning situations will vary as often as do the tasks and situations themselves. Comprehension is essentially a cognitive process and should be taught as such. Rather than teaching pupils to practice skills in a vacuum, it is more sensible to teach them how to think while selectively applying these skills to specific comprehension tasks (11).

Models suggest the teaching of a wide variety of thinking activities to promote pupil growth in comprehension. The cognitive-based models and particularly the information-processing models clearly indicate the need to develop variety and flexibility in pupils' thinking while reading. Analysis, synthesis, expectancy, and retrospection are some of the cognitive processes which models indicate are involved in comprehension. Teachers are obliged to actively teach these abilities rather than to assume that they will develop automatically as concomitants of the isolated teaching and practice of skills. In addition, the psycholinguistic models point to the importance of language and the use of language cues in comprehension. From these models, teachers can see the need to view the teaching of comprehension within the context of language learning and concept development.

Although, from a teacher's point of view, models of comprehension may be deficient in their failure to explicitly set out procedures for teaching comprehension, they do provide general principles for effective teaching. It is therefore possible to extrapolate from models to develop more effective instructional strategies for teaching comprehension.

references

1. Barrett, Thomas C. "A Taxonomy for Reading Comprehension," paper presented at the annual meeting of the International Reading Association, Anaheim, 1970.
2. Brown, Eric. "The Bases of Reading Acquisition," *Reading Research Quarterly,* 6 (Fall 1970), 49-74.
3. Carver, Ronald P. "A Computer Model of Reading and its Implications for Measurement and Research," *Reading Research Quarterly,* 6 (Summer 1971), 449-471.
4. Cleland, Donald L. "The Nature of Comprehension," *Progress and Promise in Reading.* Pittsburgh: University of Pittsburgh, 1966, 18-32.

5. Goodman, Kenneth S. "A Psycholinguistic View of Reading Comprehension," *New Frontiers in College-Adult Reading,* Fifteenth Yearbook of the National Reading Conference. Milwaukee: National Reading Conference, 1966, 188-196.

6. Goodman, Kenneth S. "Reading: A Psycholinguistic Guessing Game," in Harry Singer and Robert B. Ruddell (Eds.), *Theoretical Models and Processes of Reading.* Newark, Delaware: International Reading Association, 1970, 259-272.

7. Gray, William S. "The Major Aspects of Reading," *Sequential Development of Reading Abilities.* Chicago: University of Chicago Press, 1960, 8-24.

8. Guilford, J. P. "Three Faces of Intellect," *American Psychologist,* 14 (June 1959), 469-479.

9. Harker, W. John. "An Evaluative Summary of Models of Reading Comprehension," *Journal of Reading Behavior,* 5 (Winter 1972-1973), 26-34.

10. Harker, W. John. "Reading Comprehension to 1970: Its Theoretical and Empirical Bases, and its Implementation in Secondary Professional Textbooks, Instructional Materials, and Tests," doctoral dissertation, University of British Columbia, 1971.

11. Harker, W. John. "Teaching Comprehension: A Task Analysis Approach," *Journal of Reading,* 16 (February 1973), 379-382.

12. Holmes, Jack A. "Factors Underlying Major Reading Disabilities at the College Level," *Genetic Psychology Monographs,* 49 (January-June 1954), 3-95.

13. Holmes, Jack A. "Speed, Comprehension, and Power in Reading," *Problems, Programs, and Projects in College-Adult Reading,* Eleventh Yearbook of the National Reading Conference. Milwaukee: National Reading Conference, 1962, 6-14.

14. Jenkinson, Marion D. "Information Gaps in Research in Reading Comprehension," *Reading: Process and Pedagogy,* Nineteenth Yearbook of the National Reading Conference. Milwaukee: National Reading Conference, 1970, 179-192.

15. Kingston, Albert J. "A Conceptual Model of Reading Comprehension," *Phases of College and Other Adult Reading Programs,* Tenth Yearbook of the National Reading Conference. Milwaukee: National Reading Conference, 1961, 100-107.

16. McCullough, Constance M. "Balanced Reading Development," *Innovation and Change in Reading Instruction,* Sixty-Seventh Yearbook of the National Society for the Study of Education. Chicago: University of Chicago Press, 1968, 320-356.

17. Robinson, Helen M. "The Major Aspects of Reading," *Reading: Seventy-Five Years of Progress.* Chicago: University of Chicago Press, 1966, 22-32.

18. Ruddell, Robert B. "Psycholinguistic Implications for a Systems of Communication Model," in Kenneth S. Goodman and James T. Fleming (Eds.), *Psycholinguistics and the Teaching of Reading.* Newark, Delaware: International Reading Association, 1969, 61-78.

19. Rystrom, Richard. "Toward Defining Comprehension: A First Report," *Journal of Reading Behavior,* 2 (Winter 1970), 56-74; "Toward Defining Comprehension: A Second Report," *Journal of Reading Behavior,* 2 (Spring 1970), 144-157.

20. Simons, Herbert D. "Reading Comprehension: The Need for a New Perspective," *Reading Research Quarterly,* 6 (Spring 1971), 338-363.

21. Smith, Donald E. P. "Reading Comprehension: A Proposed Model," *Research and Evaluation in College Reading,* Ninth Yearbook of the National Reading Conference. Fort Worth: Texas Christian University Press, 1960, 21-27.

22. Spache, George D. *Toward Better Reading.* Champaign, Illinois: Garrard, 1963.

23. Stauffer, Russell G. *Directing Reading Maturity as a Cognitive Process.* New York: Harper and Row, 1969.

24. Venezky, Richard L., and Robert C. Calfee. "The Reading Competency Model," in Harry Singer and Robert B. Ruddell (Eds.), *Theoretical Models and Processes of Reading.* Newark, Delaware: International Reading Association, 1970, 273-291.

Research indicates the complex process through which beginning readers discover meaning. This process has important implications for teaching methods during the early years of instruction.

the reading process and the beginning reader: implications for the instructional program

susanna w. pflaum
university of illinois at chicago

One of the most exciting developments in the field of reading in recent years has been the appearance of conceptual models which attempt to explain the reading process. Authors such as Goodman (*8, 9*), Carroll (*3*), Crosby and Liston (*5*), Athey (*1*), Geyer (*7*), Entwhisle (*6*) and others generally stress the relatedness between language and reading. Although not all of these writers agree that this work will produce new directions for the classroom teacher, the thesis of this paper is that a focus for instruction at the beginning stages of reading acquisition can be drawn from a theoretical analysis of reading behavior. Specifically, a reformulation of Goodman's 1967 model (*9*) of the beginning reader's behavior is presented in this paper. The model is then analyzed to develop a framework for instruction. I have deliberately mixed theory and instruction against the advice of others. The reason for this mix is that, although I recognize that instruction in reading is *not* what reading is, I believe that how beginners read should provide instructional direction.

Carroll, Goodman, and Crosby and Liston agree that skilled readers engage in basically two levels of activity once visual focus has occurred. The first level is immediate perception of graphic stimuli. The second level is immediate grasp of meaning. The skilled reader continually matches visual information discovered with predictions made based on previous experience with the printed message. Among others, Hochberg and Brooks (10) point out that skilled reading is hypothesis-testing behavior. And, in his review of research and models of perception, Schiffman (12) concludes that peripheral vision provides the skilled reader with information used to direct visual focus on language cues helpful in the searching activity. Diagram A is Goodman's simplified analysis of skilled reading behavior (9).

Diagram A

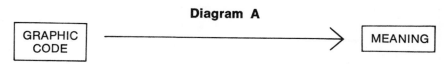

The beginning reader works much harder to achieve meaning. Many visual, auditory-related, and cognitive activities are involved as the beginner struggles through a printed message. For one thing, after naming the words, the reader must relate them to the oral language code. That is, the beginning reader who focuses on one word at a time has to put words together so that they resemble connected discourse as the reader understands it. Teachers try to help children through this particular step by urging them to read orally so that the words "sound like talk." I think it is more important for the beginner to be encouraged to hear the words as if they were talk. Thus, teachers should let children spontaneously repeat phrases and sentences as they read orally so that the words can become connected.

A preliminary step for the beginning reader is the naming of words. Automatic word recognition gradually increases during the first years of reading, but at first, the beginner must carefully search the visual stimuli for clues to each word. Diagram B represents the reading behavior of the beginner as adapted from Goodman (9).

Diagram B

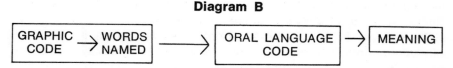

Two major additional activities occur as the beginner reads. The reader must slowly name the separate words and process the words through the oral language code to achieve meaning. Furthermore, the first step, the analysis of the graphic code so that words can be named, is a complex affair for the beginning reader.

There are a number of techniques taught to children to help them name printed words. Additionally, children use a variety of self-induced techniques, some of which are more productive than others. The first section of the above diagram has been expanded to represent major word recognition techniques in Diagram C.

Diagram C

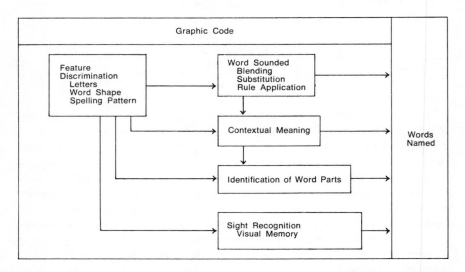

No matter what technique is used, discrimination of critical features must occur first. Depending on the explicit instruction and on the child's own induced system, the beginning reader will note the letters, the shape of the word, and/or the spelling pattern. For example, if a pure linguistic approach is the instructional system, the beginning reader will look carefully at the first letter and the spelling pattern. If the instructional system is based on high frequency vocabulary control, the reader may attend to the word shape as the discriminating feature. After perception of relevant features, the reader has a variety of possible methods to help name the printed words. Again, instructional procedures, individual flexibility, and individual learning style all influence which method or methods are actually put to use by the beginning reader.

One method is to search visual memory so that immediate sight recognition occurs. This is possible when words are treated as wholes and repetition and practice are stressed. Programs which base vocabulary control on high frequency words emphasize this method during the very early stages of reading acquisition. The assumption is that by

Implications for Instruction

focusing on sight recognition, children will become practiced in behavior typical of the skilled reader. Therefore, the stated goal of these reading programs is to develop children's stock of sight words. Although this is a logical means of looking at reading instruction, conclusions from large scale research [for example from Chall's re-examination (4) of a number of earlier studies and evidence from Bond and Dykstra's analysis (2) of the first grade reading studies] indicate that reading development is enhanced during the first year if instruction focuses on methods of relating the printed symbols with oral equivalents.

Use of phonic rules, the blending together of sounds which represent printed letters, and substitution of a sound in a familiar word pattern are alternative ways of relating printed words with their oral equivalents. These techniques are either presented to the beginner as content to be acquired or the beginner is exposed to collections of words which are highly structured to emphasize a sound-symbol relationship which the learner figures out. The beginning reader should have alternative word recognition techniques. But with some pure linguistic systems, children learn only one technique. It is important to note that, although use of phonics and linguistic methods to relate sound and print are not representative of skilled reading behavior, the beginning reader appears to profit from this training. It is much more efficient for the beginning reader to figure words independently than it is to rely on slow repetition of a smaller group of words. The reason that the use of phonics is particularly helpful for most children during the first two years of reading instruction is simply that phonics is a way of expanding the number of vocabulary words which are ultimately recognized on sight.

In addition, understanding of word modification by inflectional changes also expands the number of words recognized. And, later in reading development, children will learn to break polysyllabic words into smaller units to which they can apply phonics principles.

Another method available to the beginning reader is use of contextual clues to unlock unfamiliar words. Weber's study (13) showed that context is extensively used by first grade readers even though most programs have little explicit instruction in this technique. Weber's high-achieving first grade readers much more often spontaneously corrected their guessed words which did not "fit" the sentences being read orally than did the low-achieving first graders. This was the only critical difference in the behavior of the two groups. Weber suggested that children rely on context too much. However, her findings can be positive factors in reading acquisition. The use of context, both by itself and in combination with other word recognition techniques, should be emphasized from the beginning of reading instruction. Furthermore, all children should have explicit direction in use of context so that everyone is able to judge the value of guessed words based on individual expectations from the sentence sense.

In order to guess a word by use of context, a youngster must assess the syntactic and semantic meanings directly, make predictions based on his assessment, and then test his predictions against sentence meanings. In microcosm, the beginning reader is thus activating the hypothesis-testing behavior characteristic of the skilled reader. As the use of context is encouraged, the beginning reader learns that reading is a sensible, meaningful activity. In addition, the reader learns to rely on the oral language code to evaluate the hypothesis, rather than to rely on the teacher.

You may wonder why one would stress the value of context as a word recognition technique because of its similarity with skilled reading behavior while dismissing training in visual memory, even though instant recognition of words is also characteristic of the skilled reader. Instant recognition of many words is one goal of instruction in beginning reading, but whole-word visual memory by itself is not a very efficient way of achieving recognition of a large number of words. A heavy phonics program appears to stimulate efficient growth toward a sizeable reading vocabulary. Phonics can also be combined with contextual analysis so that sight vocabulary is increased in size and hypothesis-testing behaviors characteristic of the skilled reader are developed. For example, when the beginning reader can ask himself "What thing do I know that begins with r and fits into: *Johnny threw the r*_____ *at Billy*?" the number of possible words which fit the sentence context is reduced, compared to the same question without the information obtained by the relatedness between the printed r and the sound /r/. When both beginning and ending symbol-sound relationships are perceived and combined with contextual predictions, the number of possible words is reduced even further. As the beginning reader focuses on the salient components of the print in order to fulfill contextual prediction, he is developing the behaviors characteristic of the skilled reader.

To further emphasize these points, additions need to be made to the diagrams presented earlier. The skilled reader is continuously and progressively proceeding through the perception and meaning attainment processes. Diagram D has added a dotted arrow to represent this continuous activity.

Diagram D

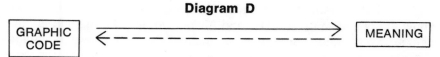

The beginning reader is also continuously moving from word perception to word naming to analysis of words through the oral code until meaning is attained. Diagram E includes all the components of the beginning reading process discussed here.

Diagram E

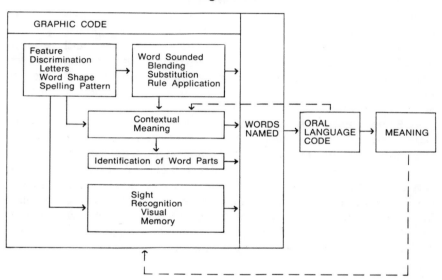

The dotted arrow at the bottom of the diagram indicates that the major activities necessary for the beginning reader to attain meaning are repeated over and over just as with the skilled reader. The dotted arrow from the oral language code to contextual meaning represents the process of word prediction and evaluation in sentence context thus demonstrating the parallel between contextual analysis and the whole reading process.

If we want the beginning reader to develop a workable and large stock of sight words as well as techniques to figure out words not in visual memory, if we desire that children from the outset expect to find meaning as they read, and if we also hope that the beginner will acquire processes which will be productive at all levels of reading achievement, then there are clear directions for instruction. Instruction in beginning reading should include these components:

1. Early reading of dictated language experience stories will show the beginner that, in Lee and Allen's words (*11*), reading is "talk written down" and therefore is as meaningful as his own language. Language experience will also provide excellent material for contextual analysis.

2. Early development of sight words will be complemented with a heavy phonics program which stresses initial single consonants and consonant clusters before work with vowels.

3. Oral exercises should introduce training in contextual word recognition. These oral exercises will be combined with auditory perception so that the beginner clearly sees how the auditory factor reduces the number of possible words which fit the context.

4. Written exercises with controlled vocabulary should be introduced as soon as reading is underway. These exercises continue the training in contextual analysis. The beginner learns from the start to evaluate his own responses in reference to the question, "Does the sentence make sense with this word?"

5. In combination with the use of initial and final consonants, word endings, and vowel patterns contextual analysis continues throughout the first two years of reading instruction with increasingly more complex sentence structures. Thus, these experiences will focus first on nouns in simple sentence patterns and slowly expand so that verbs, adjectives, articles, conjunctions, and prepositions are identified from contextual analysis. Whenever possible, the teacher will encourage the beginning reader to figure out how the words used so well in oral language can become cues in reading.

conclusion

While recognizing that instruction is not what reading is, this analysis has attempted to show that what reading is can be a framework for instructional direction. The instruction in beginning reading recommended here will not be very different from that found in some classrooms. It is hoped, however, that this discussion has presented a framework by which to analyze pupil growth and to focus instruction in word recognition techniques of maximum use to the beginning reader.

references

1. Athey, I. J. "Language Models and Reading," *Reading Research Quarterly,* Fall 1971, 18-29.
2. Bond, G. L., and Robert Dykstra. "The Cooperative Research Program in First Grade Reading Instruction," *Reading Research Quarterly,* Summer 1967, 90-142.
3. Carroll, J. P. "The Nature of the Reading Process," in L. A. Harris and C. B. Smith (Eds.), *Individualizing Reading Instruction: A Reader.* New York: Holt, Rhinehart and Winston, 1972.
4. Chall, J. *Learning to Read: The Great Debate.* New York: McGraw-Hill, 1967.
5. Crosby, R. M., and R. A. Liston. *The Waysiders: A New Approach to Reading and the Dyslexic Child.* New York: Delacorte Press, 1968.
6. Entwhisle, D. R. "Implications of Language Socialization for Reading Models and for Learning to Read," *Reading Research Quarterly,* Fall 1971, 111-167.
7. Geyer, J. J. "Comprehensive and Partial Models Related to the Reading Process," *Reading Research Quarterly,* Summer 1972, 541-587.
8. Goodman, K. S. "Behind the Eye: What Happens in Reading," *Reading: Process and Program.* Urbana, Illinois: National Council of Teachers of English, 1970.
9. Goodman, K. S. "The Psycholinguistic Nature of the Reading Process," in K. S. Goodman (Ed.), *The Psycholinguistic Nature of the Reading Process.* Detroit: Wayne State University Press, 1967.
10. Hochberg, J., and V. Brooks. "Reading As Intentional Behavior," in H. S. Singer and R. B. Ruddell (Eds.), *Theoretical Models and Processes of Reading.* Newark, Delaware: International Reading Association, 1970.
11. Lee, D. M., and R. V. Allen. *Learning to Read Through Experience.* New York: Appleton-Century-Crofts, 1963.
12. Schiffman, H. R. "Some Components of Sensation and Perception for the Reading Process," *Reading Research Quarterly,* Summer 1972, 588-612.
13. Weber, R. H. "First Graders' Use of Grammatical Context in Reading," in H. Levin and J. P. Williams (Eds.), *Basic Studies in Reading.* New York: Basic Books, 1970.

This paper offers several hypotheses dealing with the reading-decoding process and helps teachers grasp a better understanding of the reading process by explaining the relationship between comprehension and the degree of automaticity of decoding.

the comprehension process:
a focus on the beginning reader

patricia dahl
bloomington, minnesota, schools

Edmund Huey (*1*) captured the essence of the concept of automaticity sixty-five years ago when he wrote:

> To perceive an entirely new word or other combination of strokes requires considerable time, close attention, and is likely to be imperfectly done, just as when we attempt some new combination of movements, some new trick in the gymnasium or new "serve" at tennis. In either case, repetition progressively frees the mind from attention to details, makes facile the total act, shortens the time, and reduces the extent to which consciousness must concern itself with the process.

In this paper several issues relating to automaticity are discussed, such as, the effect of automatic decoding on comprehension and why one can decode accurately with little understanding of what was read.

Every person has a number of automatic behaviors in his repertoire, each of them so completely practiced that they occur at the appropriate time, in an appropriate manner, with a minimum of attention and effort. These behaviors are performed automatically until some unusual cue focuses attention on them. Walking is an automatic behavior performed without attention until a slip or near fall on a patch of ice suddenly focuses full attention on putting each foot down carefully. Driving a car can go on for long periods of time when the driver may be totally unaware of performing the task; yet he safely guides the car mile after mile perfectly executing turns, lane changes, and even stops. When attention is drawn back to the task—perhaps by some signal of possible danger—the driver often is unable to recall having passed certain landmarks, and in a state of growing anxiety may search desperately for some memory trace of having stopped at signals and marked intersections.

Although in 1908 Huey described automatic behavior in a most concise manner, and people were intuitively aware of their own automatic behaviors both before and after Huey's book was published, psychologists chose to ignore it as an investigative field until recent years. While there are numerous studies of automatic behaviors in the psychomotor literature, there are virtually no studies on automaticity in reading. The reason for this dearth of experimentation is lack of equipment and methods for measuring automatic reading behaviors.

Schmidt (3) defines *automatization* as the "dropping out of conscious cues in learning." The novice consciously goes through the steps in performing a task, while the experienced performer completes the sequence unconsciously combining each of the steps into what appears to be one fluent act. At some time, however, each of the constituting behaviors needs to be learned, practiced, and totally integrated before this smooth, effortless performance can occur. The beginning dancer watches his feet, counts steps, and consciously coordinates arm movements with the steps. After repeated practice he moves onto the floor and performs with ease and gracefulness.

Posner (2) offers a two part definition of automaticity. First is the replacement of external cues needed to guide behavior with internal cues (exteroceptive cues replaced by proprioceptive cues) and second, the process of reducing the amount of attention needed to perform a task. The skilled typist is able to listen and respond to questions while continuing to type from copy because the primary task (typing) is being guided by internalized or proprioceptive cues. The beginning typist is unable to attend to conversation because her attention is on typing. She depends on conscious cues (listening to the keys strike and visual feedback) to guide her behavior. If an error is made, its exact nature and time of occurrence is known immediately. When the skilled typist's attention is redirected to the primary task in response to proprioceptive guidance cues suddenly reporting some subtle discrepancy (a break in rhythm or a failure to make one to one correspondence with the copy) the typist must search visually for the error, which is usually found near, but not at, the point where the typing stopped.

Skilled readers decode automatically. The proficient reader cannot stop himself from reading whatever words come into his view; road signs, billboards, and titles flashed on a television screen are all read automatically. Every fluent reader was at one time a novice reader whose plight is very aptly described by Smith (4):

> Life seems particularly difficult for the beginning reader—so many necessary things are difficult for him at the outset that will be easier when his reading skills develop. For example, the mere fact that a child cannot read very fast puts a heavy burden on memory and attentional systems that are both inexperienced and overloaded with all kinds of instructions and rules.

Present conceptualizations of the skilled reading process separate the process into two parts: decoding and deriving meaning from the decoded material. Two sources of information are being processed simultaneously. Parallel processing requires consideration of two limited systems: attention and short term memory.

Attention is an all or nothing proposition. It can be shifted among different information sources, but it cannot be focused on more than one at any given time. The cocktail party phenomenon demonstrates this point. With conversations in progress all around, a listener has no difficulty in following the one conversation he chooses to hear. As interest in this conversation wanes, the listener may begin to shift attention from one to another until he finds one that, in his opinion, merits his full attention. At this point, he focuses his attention on that conversation to the exclusion of all others which are then reduced to extraneous noise.

The second system, short term memory, is limited in both the quantity of material that can be held and the length of time that material can be retained.

In the reading process, attention can be focused either on decoding or on getting meaning. When attention is focused on decoding, small bits of information, letters or letter units, are placed in short term memory. The capacity of short term memory is limited to a small number of information units. When decoding is at the letter by letter or sound unit level, only two or three short words are available at any given time. This makes association with previously learned material and past experiences necessary for long term storage very difficult, if not totally impossible. The identification of the word, then, becomes

Focus on the Beginning Reader

the end product of the process. When decoding skills are developed to the automatic level, larger units (words and phrases) are placed in short term memory, facilitating association. The maximum amount of attention is directed to obtaining meaning from the decoded material.

Whenever two behaviors occur simultaneously, at least one is being performed automatically. In reading, it seems reasonable that decoding must be the automatic behavior, and that obtaining meaning can never be automatic. In addition to the argument that larger information units must be placed in short term memory, the magnitude and nature of the two tasks preclude the possibility of automaticity in gathering meaning. Decoding is a more or less exact and finite task. The number of words in the language is large, but finite, and the words which occur with high frequency constitute a relatively small percentage of the total number. Once effortless recognition of high frequency words is accomplished, attention can be directed away from the decoding process. Gathering meaning is a constructive and infinite task. The receiver of information must actively construct the meaning of the decoded words through constantly relating and associating the new material with previous knowledge. The number of meanings that words in different combinations and contexts can carry is nearly limitless.

Although automaticity in decoding is a necessary prerequisite for gathering meaning, it does not guarantee understanding. Often a reader decodes several pages without gaining meaning because attention has been directed elsewhere. Automatic decoding frees attention which then must be intentionally directed toward comprehending the written language.

Obviously, changing the beginning reader into a proficient reader is the ultimate goal of all reading instruction from preprimer readiness lessons to the termination of formal instruction. The real task of the teacher of reading is to develop automatic decoding in the students.

Developing automaticity in decoding skills is simply giving practice beyond accuracy. To be able to identify the words is not enough; the student needs instantaneous recognition. He needs to practice until he can say the word as quickly as it can be presented. As soon as the child achieves a sight vocabulary of ten words, he should practice them over and over again. As new words are added to the students' sight vocabulary, they need to be added to the practice set. The key to automaticity in a skill is repeated practice on already accurate behaviors.

The methods used in achieving repeated practice are limited only by the teacher's imagination and resources. Words can be presented on index cards, flash cards, or on slides. This repeated practice does not need to be limited to recognizing words in isolation. During the colonial period of our history, mothers were the reading teachers. They used whatever books happened to be in the household—the Bible, a prayer book, or the catechism. Often there was only one book for the child to use for practice, so he read the same material over and over again. With this repeated practice on familiar material, the child read with increasing speed, decreasing errors, and decreasing effort —in other words, his reading became automatic. Certainly, no one would advocate teaching reading by practicing in only one book year after year, but reading the same mastered material over and over again as an adjunct to ongoing reading instruction could become another method of achieving effortless decoding.

The principles of attention and automaticity can be used to explain the "word caller," a phenomenon which has perplexed teachers for a long time. Teachers have wondered how a child can accurately decode the words on the page and yet comprehend so little of the meaning contained therein. The word caller is usually a child who is not automatic in decoding, but is accurate in word recognition. The reader's attention is on the mechanics of reading and his reading rate is slow. Thus, there is an overload on the child's attentional and short term memory systems, which interferes with accessing meaning.

We have seen in this paper how the principles of attention and automaticity may be used to explain why the skilled reader is able to derive meaning from the printed page, whereas the beginning reader, though accurate in decoding, may have difficulty in understanding what has been read.

references

1. Huey, Edmund Burke. *The Psychology and Pedagogy of Reading.* Cambridge, Massachusetts: M.I.T. Press, 1968.
2. Posner, Michael I. "Reduced Attention and the Performance of 'Automated' Movements," *Journal of Motor Behavior,* 1 (1969), 245-258.
3. Schmidt, Richard A. "Anticipation and Timing in Human Motor Performance," *Psychological Bulletin,* 70 (1968), 631-646.
4. Smith, Frank. *Understanding Reading—A Psycholinguistic Analysis of Reading and Learning To Read.* New York: Holt, Rinehart and Winston, 1971, 3.

This study compares the cloze method with the Dale-Chall formula in determining readability using elementary science textbook materials.

cloze readability versus the dale-chall formula

victor froese
university of manitoba

Much contradictory evidence is found in the literature with regard to the measurement of readability. Some of the most pertinent findings concerning the readability of elementary science textbook materials are examined in this paper.

Since, by generally accepted standards, a readability formula is applicable only to material similar to the criterion on which it was based (3, 10), it appears that the Dale-Chall formula scores for elementary science textbooks material should be used cautiously. In 1958, Chall stated that no studies had been reported that were based exclusively on the specialized subject matters of science or mathematics. A search of the literature to date reveals no validation studies on elementary science materials.

Several studies, however, show findings based on the application of the Dale-Chall formula to materials which were not included in the original or subsequent validations. This practice would lead one to question the results of these studies.

Brown (2) questions the appropriateness of the Dale list of 3,000 familiar words as a vocabulary load factor in the Dale-Chall formula. He found that students at the seventh and eighth grade levels apparently comprehended a NSTA publication entitled *Spacecraft* which was rated at eleventh to twelfth grade level by the Dale-Chall formula. Furthermore, when the vocabulary from a 1961 edition of a third grade science textbook was accepted as familiar, it was found that it lowered the readability of the same sample from eleventh to twelfth grade level to ninth to tenth grade level. He concluded that when the Dale-Chall formula was applied to science textbooks it seemed to place them higher than was warranted.

Walker (*18*) used the Dale-Chall formula to evaluate thirty-nine commercially produced programed textbooks for grades four to six and found that the Dale-Chall readability levels for these books were consistently higher than the grade levels assigned to them by the publisher. Sixty-seven percent of the books were rated above the grade level indicated by the publisher, and three of the books had no samples at the intermediate level. This type of finding may be questioned since the variability may be due to either the nature of the formula or the material being evaluated. Although high relationships among the Fry, Lorge, Flesch, and Dale-Chall formulas are reported by Fry (*4*), contradictory evidence is quoted by Michaelis and Tyler (*13*). Marshall (*12*) finds no significant relationship between readability and comprehension when using the Flesch Reading Ease formula on high school physics books.

Since most of the formulas are based on common or highly interrelated factors, and since the vocabulary factor accounts for a very substantial amount of the variance of readability elements, this aspect of the formulas must be examined for its contribution toward formula consistency or inconsistency. There is also some evidence to indicate that vocabulary difficulty is a better predictor at lower levels of difficulty (*3*) and for poorer readers (*5*).

The Winnetka, Dale-Tyler, Gray-Leary, Lorge, Dale-Chall, Dolch, and Spache formulas all use basic word lists which are dated since they were compiled in the 1920s and 1930s. Evidence gathered by Stone (*15*) and Jacobs (*7*) indicates that vocabularies have changed. Kucera and Francis (*6*) also found that of the Dolch 220 words of the 1920s, 82 words (37 percent) were not among their 1960 compilation of the most frequently used 220 words. Recognizing the possibility that this change might affect the readability, Spache has now adopted Stone's revised list. The validity of the other formulas, however, could be questioned since their lists have not been revised.

Bormuth (*1*), in investigating a measure of word depth as a predictor of comprehension difficulty in literature, science, and history materials, found that it predicts differences in comprehension of different subject matter written at the same readability level. This led him to suggest:

In the past the assumption has been that such differences were caused by differences inherent in the content of the subject matters themselves. Though this concept has never been rigorously defined, it is given the labels of concept difficulty or idea density.

In other words, he is questioning differences in readability commonly attributed to the content areas.

In her 1958 summary of readability research, Chall (3) states the need for cross-validation research into textbook materials:

Most of the existing validation studies have been on juvenile fiction. Since the formulas are used by educational publishers and textbook committees for evaluating textbooks for a particular grade, we need to know how valid the predicted grade-placement indexes of the various formulas are when compared to tested comprehension or to teacher or pupil judgment of difficulty.

In his 1963 investigation of readability research, Klare (8) proposes the following areas for future research which are related to this study: The use of new word lists, specialized word lists, specialized lists for specialized purposes, longer lists, criterion passage refinement, when or where to use specific formulas, and separate norms for the readability of different types of materials and audiences.

It is apparent that the Dale-Chall formula has not been validated on elementary science materials. The Dale list of 3,000 familiar words may be questioned for relevance to science material. And the weighting of the vocabulary factor in the formula may need adjustment for certain types of materials or for certain levels of materials.

Furthermore, differences in readability due to content materials have been questioned. Also some contradictory evidence about the relationship between readability and comprehension has been presented. Finally, a need for readability research with respect to validation and to the use of word lists and content material has been expressed.

Further research, especially on the validity of using the Dale-Chall formula on elementary science textbook material, therefore, is needed.

the problem

This study was designed to investigate the problem: How valid are the Dale-Chall readability ratings for sixth grade science textbook materials when compared to an independent criterion of language difficulty expressed in cloze units?

null hypothesis

There is no significant difference between the correlation coefficient of .90 obtained in the original cross-validation of the Dale-Chall Readability Formula and the coefficient of correlation between the Dale-Chall readability ratings and the mean cloze score obtained by the subjects completing the cloze test over randomly selected sixth grade science textbook passages.

definition of terms

1. *Cross-Validation.* A comparison of a predicted readability level to an independent criterion of readability (or language difficulty).

2. *Cloze Procedure* (or *Cloze technique*). A method of intercepting a message from a transmitter, mutilating its language patterns by deleting parts [in this case, every fifth word] and so administering it to receivers that their attempts to make the pattern whole again yields a number of cloze units [the score] (*16*).

3. *Independent Criterion of Language Difficulty.* A measure of the language difficulty of a passage expressed in mean cloze units for the subjects having read a particular passage.

4. *Readability.* A prediction of the ease or difficulty with which written material may be comprehended according to the specified criteria.

5. *Sixth Grade Science Textbook Materials.* Randomly selected samples of science materials from textbook series designated for the sixth grade by the publisher and listed in *Textbooks in Print 1968* (*17*).

the population

The sample under study consisted of 366 randomly selected sixth grade students enrolled in thirteen classrooms in eleven different schools in School District #33, Chilliwack, British Columbia, Canada. The 366 students represented approximately one-half of the sixth grade students in this district.

The mean Canadian Lorge-Thorndike IQ (*11*) for the 366 students was 102 with a standard deviation of 15. Approximately 51 percent were girls and approximately 49 percent were boys.

The Canadian Test of Basic Skills (*9*), subtest Vocabulary and Comprehension, were administered sixty days before this study and resulted in a mean score of 6.19 (SD = 1.27) and 6.15 (SD = 1.26), respectively.

Both the IQ and Basic Skills tests were administered as a regular part of the district testing program.

summary of findings

Four specific findings were obtained from the data in this study:

1. The twelve cloze passages used in this study yielded a mean reliability coefficient of .79 with a range of .64 to .89. These coefficients are comparable to some standardized group reading tests.

2. The cloze scores obtained for each passage correlated from .55 to .85 with intelligence as measured by the Canadian Lorge-Thorndike test. These coefficients are comparable to those found in studies by Hafner and Jenkinson (14).

3. The cloze scores obtained for each passage correlated from .64 to .86 with reading vocabulary and from .52 to .85 with reading comprehension. These findings compare favorably with those cited by Rankin (14).

4. The cross-validation coefficient of .90 obtained by Dale and Chall and the cross-validation coefficient of —.29 obtained in this study are significantly different beyond the .01 level of confidence.

limitations

The findings and conclusions in this study must be interpreted while keeping in mind the relatively small number of passages, the reliability and validity of the cloze tests, the specific samples of subjects, and the science material used:

1. An item sampling error was probably inherent in the cloze passages.

2. Approximately 55 percent of the passages were within the frustration levels of the examinees completing the passages. This factor could cause a leveling off of the distribution of scores for the cloze passages at the upper end of difficulty.

conclusions

Subject to the limitations of this study, the following four conclusions were drawn from the findings:

1. The cloze tests are reliable measures of language difficulty when used for group testing.

2. The cloze tests are valid measures of language difficulty as demonstrated by their concurrent validity with intelligence test scores.

Table of Data for Twelve Randomly Selected Elementary Science Textbook Passages

Passage Number	Mean Cloze Score	Cloze Standard Deviation	Corrected Split-half Reliability	Dale-Chall Readability Index	Correlation of Cloze and Intelligence	Correlation of Cloze and Vocabulary	Correlation of Cloze and Comprehension
1	16.45	6.17	.82	7.06	.67	.74	.64
2	15.78	5.04	.73	6.90	.85	.86	.85
3	18.40	4.78	.67	7.45	.55	.78	.79
4	12.30	5.75	.64	6.82	.62	.65	.66
5	18.08	6.45	.83	5.17	.67	.64	.58
6	19.90	5.11	.89	6.92	.66	.67	.71
7	17.10	6.01	.82	6.91	.75	.77	.76
8	11.65	4.69	.80	7.70	.63	.64	.63
9	20.48	6.35	.82	8.01	.65	.79	.73
10	13.27	3.73	.75	8.38	.61	.64	.52
11	19.00	5.71	.73	5.54	.76	.82	.79
12	15.82	4.24	.64	6.33	.66	.83	.79

Determining Readability

3. The cloze tests are valid measures of language difficulty as demonstrated by their congruent validity with reading vocabulary and reading comprehension scores.

4. The Dale-Chall Readability Formula is not a valid measure of sixth grade science textbook materials when the cloze procedure is used as a criterion.

implications

Since the null hypothesis was rejected, and since the Dale-Chall Readability Formula was found not to be a valid measure of sixth grade science material, the following implications should be considered:

1. Previous research using the Dale-Chall Readability Formula on elementary science textbook materials should be reexamined.

2. In order to validly measure science materials with the Dale-Chall Readability Formula the following alterations may be necessary: a) weighting the formula differently, b) compiling a specialized word list, c) updating the word list, d) developing special norms, or e) some combination of these.

3. For some purposes, such as matching a book to a reader, the cloze procedure may be a more robust and parsimonious measure of language difficulty than the Dale-Chall Readability Formula.

4. Research using passages written specifically for a certain Dale-Chall readability level should be interpreted cautiously since this practice has, in effect, eliminated the readability measurement error. This result could lead to different conclusions from those indicated when randomly selected passages are subjected to a readability formula.

5. This study should be replicated at the same and at other grade levels, with differing populations, and with other randomly selected science textbook passages.

references

1. Bormuth, J. R. "Mean Word Depth as a Predictor of Comprehension Difficulty," *California Journal of Educational Research,* 15 (November 1964), 226-231.

2. Brown, W. R. "Science Textbook Selection and the Dale-Chall Formula," *School Science and Mathematics,* 65 (February 1965), 164-167.

3. Chall, J. S. *Readability: An Appraisal of Research and Application,* Bureau of Educational Research Monographs, No. 34. Columbus, Ohio: 1958, 35, 45, 165.

4. Fry, E. "A Readability Formula that Saves Time," *Journal of Reading,* 11 (April 1968), 513-516.

5. Holmes, J. A., and H. Singer. *Speed and Power of Reading in High School,* Bureau of Educational Research and Development. Washington, D.C.: U.S. Government Printing Office, 1966, 104-109.

6. Johnson, D. D. "The Dolch List Reexamined," *Reading Teacher,* 24 (February 1971), 449-457.

7. Jacobs, H. D. "A Replicative Investigation of the Buchingham-Dolch Free-Association Word Study," doctoral dissertation, University of Oregon, 1967.

8. Klare, G. R. *The Measurement of Readability.* Ames, Iowa: Iowa State University Press, 1963, 189-190.

9. King, E. M., E. F. Lindquist, and A. N. Heironymous. *Canadian Test of Basic Skills,* Test V: Vocabulary and Test R: Reading Comprehension. Toronto, Ontario: Thomas Nelson and Sons, 1968.

10. Lorge, Irving. "Readability Formulae—An Evaluation," *Elementary English,* 26 (February 1949), 87-88.

11. Lorge, I., et al. *Canadian Lorge-Thorndike Intelligence Tests,* Level D, Verbal. Toronto, Ontario: Thomas Nelson and Sons, 1968.

12. Marshall, J. S. "Comprehension and Alleged Readability of High School Physics Textbooks," *Science Education,* 46 (October 1962), 335-346.

13. Michaelis, J. U., and F. T. Tyler. "A Comparison of Reading Ability and Readability," *Journal of Educational Psychology,* 52 (1951), 491-498.

14. Rankin, E. F. "The Cloze Procedure—A Survey of Research," in E. L. Thurston and L. E. Hafner (Eds.), *The Philosophical and Sociological Bases of Reading,* Fourteenth Yearbook of the National Reading Conference. Milwaukee, Wisconsin: 1965, 133-150.

15. Stone, C. R. "Measuring Difficulty of Primary Reading Material: A Constructive Criticism of Spache's Measure," *Elementary School Journal,* 57 (October 1956), 36-41.

16. Taylor, W. L. "Cloze Procedure: A New Tool for Measuring Readability," *Journalism Quarterly,* 30 (1953), 416.

17. *Textbooks in Print 1968.* New York: R. R. Bowker, 1968, 217-250.

18. Walker, W. L. "Measured Readability of Intermediate Grade Textbooks," *Teachers College Journal,* 37 (March 1966), 179-181.

Although variability in reading difficulty is not an exclusive problem of the math content area, the use of this subject area as an example directs attention toward the evaluation of content area difficulties.

readability interference in reading mathematics texts

betty willmon
tallahassee, florida

One curriculum area which is rapidly changing is that of mathematics. The change has affected mathematics teaching at all grade levels. From the reports of a survey of new materials it appears that, in the haste to publish mathematics textbooks, slight attention has been given to readability levels and, in particular, to their technical vocabulary load.

Modern math teaching begins as early as or before the first grade. Unless authors take great care, the vocabulary burden can become very high and interfere with concept learning, since the primary grade years is the time when the student's general reading vocabulary learning is proportionately the heaviest of his life. Thus, it seems imperative for all teachers involved—not only math teachers but also those responsible for the teaching of reading—to include arithmetic vocabulary in the general curriculum.

Research literature indicates that many problems in mathematics are due to reading difficulties (2, 4, 8). Readability studies of math textbooks (3, 5, 7) indicate that the technical vocabulary load may be the source of some major reading problems. A recent mathematics word frequency count of 24 current first, second, and third grade textbooks reveals that the number of terms introduced in the primary grades is 473 (*11*). These findings suggest that mathematics terminology may be unduly large for average readers in grades one, two, and three. This study implies that the number of new words and the rate of introduction in primary arithmetic materials may be too great for textbooks to be the sole teaching vehicles and that supplementary mathematical vocabulary study is needed for effective mathematics teaching.

problem

The specific purpose of this study was to determine the relative difficulty, in terms of frequency of use, of the 473 technical words and terms occurring in mathematics textbooks, grades one to three (*11*). The questions answered were: What percent of the most frequently used math words and terms are not on the Thorndike-Lorge most frequently used 500 list? What percent of the most frequently used math terms are not on the Thorndike-Lorge most frequently used 1000 list? What percent are not introduced in basal reading series until grade four or later?

The general purpose of this study was to: 1) provide an instructional source for those teachers preparing supplementary mathematics materials for instruction, 2) prepare a vocabulary checklist for use in the reading program, and 3) indicate which words and terms from the most frequently used math list probably will not be introduced in the child's primary grade reading program.

background

Much of the research concerning reading problems in mathematics has focused in the area of readability. Researchers have encountered certain problems: The reading levels of many mathematics books appear too high for the target population (7), and many of the readability formulas are inappropriate for estimating the difficulty of mathematics teaching materials (5).

Smith and Heddens (7) report readability problems with primary grade math textbooks. They point out that new methods and materials are irrelevant if the student cannot read his text. Many of the new experimental mathematics materials require more reading than traditional materials. Employing the Spache Readability Formula on primary materials, Smith and Heddens report that the readability levels tend to be too high for many third grade students. In interpreting the range of readability it appears that, although the readability of some material averages out at a certain grade level, portions of the books are excessively difficult. The Dale-Chall Formula was applied at the intermediate level where a considerably higher readability level was found than at the assigned grade level. Many portions of fourth grade materials had a readability level as high as tenth grade, and portions of fifth and sixth grade materials, as high as twelfth grade level.

Issues involved in utilizing readability formulas with mathematical books are discussed by Kane (5). Certain words with specific math meanings may appear on one vocabulary list but may not appear on vocabulary lists from which readability studies are reproduced.

The technical jargon of mathematics of symbol systems and phrases presents still another hindrance in applying readability techniques. The fault does not lie with the readability techniques. Kane (5) thinks it lies with the inappropriate applications of the contexts for which they were not designed. He also found that there are no readability formulas based exclusively on materials devoted to specialized areas such as science and mathematics.

Willmon, in a review of the research in primary reading problems in mathematics, reports five word frequency studies. The studies varied in procedures and tabulation; however, conclusions of the researchers follow: 1) if all basal reading vocabulary is mastered, students will still require mathematics vocabulary study; 2) the number of words is unnecessarily large; 3) transient children may have difficulty with words not reviewed; 4) teachers need word lists since publishers do not supply them; and 5) there is a lack of repetition and reinforcement. Willmon recommends that supplementary materials for teaching mathematical vocabulary be developed and used (11).

method

The procedure followed in this study was to divide the most frequently used math terms into seven classes, based on frequency of use.

A comparison between classes was made to determine which words were on the Thorndike-Lorge 500 and 1000 Word Lists (10). A second comparison between classes was conducted from the Revised Core Vocabulary list of words introduced in basal reading series (9).

The percentage of those math words and terms appearing on the lists was determined. Percentages were calculated in order to find the percentage of words not likely to be taught in a primary grade reading program and to determine the relative difficulty, according to the frequency of use, of each word.

results

Table I presents a summary of the findings. There is a systematic decrease in the percentage of math words which occur on lists with the frequency which was encountered in this study. The standard reading lists, therefore, appear to give qualitative agreement with the word list in this study.

The total of percentages of technical terms not appearing on the Thorndike-Lorge 500 List is 84 percent. The percentage of math terms appearing on this list is less than 50 percent in all but two individual word frequency classes. Of the 473 math terms, 396 are not on the 500 list.

The total of percentages of technical terms not appearing on the Thorndike-Lorge 1000 List is 69 percent. The percentage of math terms appearing on this list is less than 50 percent in all but three individual word frequency classes. Of the 473 math terms, 225 are not on the 1000 list.

The total of percentages of technical terms not appearing on the Basal Reader List is 54 percent. The percentage of math terms appearing on this list is less than 50 percent in all but four individual word frequency classes. Of the 473 math items, 255 are not on the Basal Reader List.

In all cases, the percentages of the total number of words not found on the standard lists (500, 1000, and Basal) are significantly larger than the mean of the individual percentages. This result strongly indicates that the infrequently used words in the mathematics texts are even more infrequently used in common reading vocabulary.

discussion

The results of the comparisons support the findings reported in the earlier math word frequency count study by Willmon (11). She found that the total number of different mathematical terms introduced in the primary grades appears to be too great for textbooks to be the sole teaching vehicles. The comparisons between lists reveal that more math terms are introduced in the basal reading series than are on the Thorndike-Lorge 1000 List. Also, studies continue to show limited instruction in the area of content reading in basal reading series

Table 1 Math Words and Terms

Frequency of Usage	Number of Words	Words on T-L 500 List	% of Words Not on T-L 500 List	Words on T-L 1000 List	% of Words Not on T-L 1000 List	Words on Basal List	% of Words Not on Basal List
> 1000	17	11	35%	13	24%	13	24%
< 1000 > 500	27	15	44%	19	30%	19	30%
< 500 > 100	122	43	65%	71	42%	79	35%
< 100 > 50	58	13	78%	25	57%	29	50%
< 50 > 35	38	7	82%	13	66%	16	58%
< 35 > 25	39	6	85%	10	74%	13	69%
< 25	172	22	87%	37	78%	49	78%
Totals	473	77	84%	148	69%	218	54%

(1). The comparisons conducted in this study suggest the infrequently used math terms should be introduced in math textbooks with extreme care since their usage may not be reinforced by other sources. This factor appears to be an important reason for preparing word frequency tables for each of the subject areas and revising them as the curriculum changes. In addition, it is recommended that teachers use the 473 Math Word List (11) to prepare vocabulary reinforcement materials in the instructional reading program.

references

1. Austin, Mary. *The Torch Lighters.* Cambridge: Harvard University Press, 1961.
2. Eagle, Edwin. "The Relationship of Certain Reading Abilities to Success in Mathematics," *Mathematics Teacher,* 41 (April 1948), 175-179.
3. Johnson, Donovan. "The Readability of Mathematics Textbooks," *Mathematics Teacher,* 50 (February 1957), 105-110.
4. Johnson, H. C. "The Effect of Instruction in Mathematical Vocabulary Upon Problem Solving in Arithmetic," *Journal of Educational Research,* 38 (March 1945), 481-498.
5. Kane, Robert B. "The Readability of Mathematics Textbooks," paper presented at the National Council of Mathematics, Milwaukee, 1969.
6. Kerfoot, James F. "The Vocabulary in Primary Arithmetic Texts," *Reading Teacher,* 14 (January 1961), 177-180.
7. Smith, J. K., and J. W. Heddens. "The Readability of Experimental Mathematics Materials," *Arithmetic Teacher,* 11 (October 1964), 391-394.
8. Streby, George. "Reading in Mathematics," *Arithmetic Teacher,* 4 (March 1957), 79-81.
9. Taylor, Stanford et al. *A Revised Core Vocabulary.* Huntington, New York: Educational Developmental Laboratories, 1969.
10. Thorndike, Edward L., and Irving Lorge. *The Teacher's Word Book of 30,000 Words.* New York: Teachers College Press, 1944.
11. Willmon, Betty. "Reading in the Content Area: A New Math Terminology List for the Primary Grades," *Elementary English,* 50 (May 1971).

One measure of the reading difficulty of material is the number of idioms the material contains. A research study documenting this conclusion is described and the implications of this research for reading programs should be noted.

the effect of idioms on children's reading and understanding of prose

peter edwards
university of british columbia

The English language, which had its origins in the Indo-European language family, has been strongly influenced by several other languages during its evolutionary development. Modern English is characterized, among other things, by its facility to absorb new items of vocabulary. Over the centuries, numerous words and word combinations have been adapted to the English tongue through usage. A good example of this is illustrated by the number of acronyms which have become recognized as legitimate words in the English language since World War II. Words such as *radar* (*r*adio *d*etection *a*nd *r*anging) which is also a palindrome, and *laser* (*l*ight *a*mplification by *s*timulated *e*mission of *r*adiation), began as terms constructed from the initial letters of a descriptive phrase. Then, because of their rapid acceptance and widespread use by the English-speaking public, these acronyms became an established part of Standard English.

Many other variations of English usage, however, are not classified as Standard English. The following will serve to illustrate this point:

> *Example 1*   "Oh struth, cobber! Come off it! You mean that the
> geezer down at the Johnny Horner in the bag of fruit
> is really your china plate?"

Example 2   "What'll happen to the broad?"
"She'll be sent up the river."
"Ya sure?"
"Five will get you ten, pal."
"How about if she comes clean?"
"Look, she's a two time loser already."
"Come on. She's on the up and up."
"O.K! O.K!"

Perhaps in the future, certain aspects of slang usage will become an accepted part of the English language, but usually this form of expression is rarely written and is used predominantly at a restricted colloquial level of speech.

There are, however, some highly unusual patterns of English language called idioms, which are common, widely used, and accepted as part of Standard English:

English Language Idioms

fly in the ointment
jump at an offer
hit it off with someone
live from hand to mouth
lick into shape
leave someone cold
take issue with
wild goose chase
crow about something
be at loose ends
lose face
over their head
be in the running
steal the show
take someone in
red-letter day
off the top of one's head
draw the line

What do we mean then by *idiom, slang,* and *Standard English?* For the purposes of this discussion the following definitions will apply:

Idioms
Idioms refer to expressions or phrases which are peculiar to a given language and which carry either a literal meaning or a non-literal meaning depending on the intent of the writer. In other words, idioms (as the term is used here) are ambiguous, and to

Effect of Idioms

be understood they must be known either as a unit or deduced from the context. That is, the intended meaning cannot be arrived at by literal analysis (e.g. "He kicked the bucket" can literally mean just that, but it usually conveys its idiomatic meaning, "he died.").

Slang
The use of this term will refer to colloquial words or phrases not regarded as Standard English.

Standard English
This term will represent the written dialect of the educated users of the language and will include idioms but will not include slang.

In an attempt to determine the effect of idioms on children's reading and understanding of prose, the main aspects of a study conducted by the writer at the University of British Columbia will be presented.

background and statement of the problem

There is considerable evidence in educational research to show that a great many normal children have difficulty in understanding what they read. This study was designed to test one reason why the reading difficulty may occur.

Several researchers (3, 6) have pointed out the vital role of idioms in the English language. A number of recent classroom studies have illustrated the incidence of idioms in school texts and have suggested the need to teach idiomatic language as part of English language programs in schools.

A Selection of Idioms Taken from Various School Textbooks

Elementary
Level 2   pick up the scent
no time to lose
hide the panic
in no time
pick up a trail

Level 3   catch them off guard
held his breath
breezed through
mental storehouse
key players

Junior	took stock of his ideas
Secondary	he cleaned up in the deal
	the right kind of head
	not to my taste
	blood ran cold
	drummed out of the army
	blood stood still
	candle was fully spent

Very few research projects, however, have concentrated on the effect of idioms on the ability of a child to understand a passage of prose.

By the time a child enters formal education in the elementary school he "displays language performance which reflects a high degree of competence" (8). That is, most first graders can converse and process or understand what is being said to them. They understand sentence patterns and a variety of transformations; such as, commands, statements, questions, and embedded sentences. Strickland (9) observed that children exhibited far greater skill in using language patterns than was previously realized.

Reading, however, is not merely word-calling. A perceptual process must accompany the deciphering of graphic symbols. Dechant (4) stated this admirably when he referred to the complete reading act as being an involvement in which the reader brings meaning to the printed symbols through his cultural and experiential background. The perceptual process involves seeing the printed word, recognizing the word, understanding its meaning, and relating the word to its context.

But what if an adequate knowledge of vocabulary depends on what Pei (7) refers to as an understanding of stale metaphors, similes, and idioms, which in the words of George Orwell, "construct your sentences for you . . . think your thoughts for you . . . and conceal your meaning even from yourself"? In effect, if we use Chomsky's model of deep sentence structures transforming experiences into phonological or graphological surface units, the reader must be able to choose the correct interpretation even when the sentence is truly idiomatic and therefore ambiguous (10).

The problem is exacerbated if the child does not have a satisfactory home environment where he is exposed to a wide variety of language and reading experiences. Ruddell (8) mentioned the fact that a young person's language comprehension is directly related to his strategies and objects. If the child has had little or no experience in identifying and understanding the complexities of idiomatic language, he will be at a disadvantage when confronted with idioms in reading material. As mentioned earlier, a good understanding of metaphors will usually help alleviate this difficulty. Familiarity with idioms and metaphors will also enable a young person to cope more effectively with the changing nature of the English language.

Idiomatic expressions in reading material pose further difficulties when adults write books for children without first making a careful study of the prevailing modes of popular language usage. The successful author, Maria Wotzchowski, maintained that writing children's books should be attempted only by writers who can appreciate the needs and abilities of their young readers. This latter point is extremely important because in the case of idioms we invariably do not mean anything like the words we use. Chafe's comment (2) that speakers are aware of literalizations and the relation between idioms and their literal counterparts is interesting to consider at this stage. Chafe's point is that if the encoder of the language were not aware of the confusion caused by idioms, "many puns would be impossible to create and appreciate, and literature would be a very different and much duller thing than it is." Surely, this is the issue! What if children don't follow the use of idiomatic language? What indeed does happen to communication and literary appreciation? Bolinger (1) appears to make the same faulty generalization. He states that the essence of syntax is choice, and the main consideration one should have for his audience is the fact that syntax will follow clearly defined rules. Again it would seem that idioms remain an uncontrolled variable.

The purpose of this study was to determine whether idioms cause children to experience difficulty when reading prose. A test containing a number of idioms which are in common usage in English prose was constructed and administered to randomly assigned eighth grade students. It was then argued that the inclusion of idiomatic expressions into prose content caused difficulty in understanding for the students as measured by the number of correct responses to the questions asked about the passages.

selection of classes and assignment of treatments

In order to test the hypothesis and answer the question posed, the study was conducted in two secondary schools in the North Vancouver area, with four classes randomly selected from each school.

One hundred and twenty-eight eighth grade children were used from each of the two schools. The children were selected from heterogeneously grouped classes and were not classified as academic, vocational, or occupational students.

The general mental ability of the students was measured by the Lorge-Thorndike scale, and the scores were recorded. The Lorge-Thorndike scale has been used by North Vancouver schools for some time, so standardized scores were available for all students.

A table of random numbers was used to assign the students equally into four experimental conditions within each class. Thus, IQ and sex were randomly distributed over the four tests.

All students received a set of eighteen passages of prose, the same for each experimental condition, except as follows:

Nonliteral 1 (NL_1) All passages contained idiomatic language. These were the original eighteen passages chosen.

Nonliteral 2 (NL_2) The same eighteen passages except that six of them were rewritten in literal English.

Nonliteral 3 (NL_3) The same eighteen passages except that twelve of them were rewritten in literal English.

Literal (LIT) All eighteen of the passages were rewritten in literal English.

The sets of prose were made into test booklets and questions were asked about each prose selection. In order to answer the questions correctly, the students were required to have an understanding of the idiomatic expressions, or literal counterparts, in context. Four alternatives *(a, b, c, d)* were given for each passage. The alternatives were expressed in literal English and were identical for the four sets. If the students didn't agree with any of the choices being offered, they were told to write next to *e* the answer they considered to be the best.

measurement condition

The reading passages were timed to ensure that students could complete the work in a normal school period. The schools used in the study were checked to ensure that the class periods were uniform and of adequate duration. As an added precaution, a pilot study was conducted in another school having the same period length as the schools used in the study, to ensure that the tasks could be completed in the time available.

The test booklets were given at similar times in each school. The study was carried out in late January, as by that time the children had settled down after the Christmas holidays and were not distracted by impending exams.

The test booklets were constructed to look like normal class exercises. No mention of the terms *literal* or *nonliteral* was made at any time during the testing. Regular staff members conducted the tests in each school employing instructions that were standard for all groups.

Reading materials used in the test booklets were selected from, or were similar to, resource materials designed for use by eighth grade students in British Columbia schools.

design

The main analytic technique was a one-way ANOVA to test the hypothesis that nonliteral passages of prose would be more difficult to understand than literal passages.

results

The means for all treatment groups and the means for boys and girls are presented in Tables 1 and 2.

analysis of variance

The hypothesis stated that nonliteral passages of prose would be more difficult for children to understand than comparable passages

Table 1   Means for all treatment groups

Treatment	NL_1	NL_2	NL_3	LIT
Mean	13.00	13.58	14.47	15.59

Table 2   Treatment means for boys and girls

Treatment	NL_1	NL_2	NL_3	LIT
Boys	12.92	13.30	14.54	15.47
Girls	13.10	13.78	14.35	15.72

Table 3   Summary of Analysis of Variance

Source of Variation	d.f.	S.S.	M.S.	F	P
Treatment	3	245.43	81.81	23.24	.00001
Within cells (error)	252	887.025	3.52		
Total	255	1132.455			

$F_{3,252} = 23.24$ $F_{3,252; .95} = 2.65$

of literal prose. The summary of the analysis of variance is in Table 3. On the basis of these results, the null hypothesis was rejected.

conclusions

The main purpose of this study was to attempt to determine whether idioms had an adverse effect on children's reading and understanding of prose. A highly significant effect was found. The results of the study also showed that there was a positive relationship between the incidence of idioms in the test material and the amount of difficulty experienced by the children. Further, the effect seemed not to depend on sex and, although children with high IQs had less difficulty than those with low IQs, this held equally at all levels of idiomaticity.

The assumption can be made, therefore, that children who lack an understanding of idioms and yet are asked to read material containing numerous idiomatic expressions will experience difficulty unless they can utilize other techniques such as context clues to gain understanding.

limitations

The findings of this study can be applied only to the student body from which the subjects were randomly chosen. Replication of the study in other areas would be valuable to establish whether the effects obtained are general or local.

Eighteen idioms were used in the tests. This number was chosen to enable three variations of the original test to be constructed. Other multiples of three could have been used, but it was decided to concentrate on eighteen items which exhibited good content validity and which could conveniently be administered in the time available to the investigator.

The item stems were brief and were designed merely to facilitate an overall understanding of the passage which contained either the idiom or its literal counterpart.

Because of the brevity of the test stems, the student was unable to gain much assistance from context clues.

The items containing idioms were evenly spaced throughout the tests in which they appeared. No attempt was made to experiment with other arrangements or combinations of idiomatic and literal items.

Effect of Idioms

discussion

The author feels that it would be unfair to label children as "poor readers" without first defining the type of reading material they are using. Children who can function adequately when reading literal English (as defined in this study) should receive praise and encouragement. These youngsters should then be motivated to continue to the next phase of their reading experience—that of Standard English which includes idioms.

This situation has particular meaning for children from minority groups who lack an understanding of the cultural background expressed in most of the books that they read. There are, however, many disadvantaged children who are not members of a minority group and they also need attention in this regard.

implications

Several areas for further research are indicated by the results of this study.

A great deal needs to be known about the incidence and type of idiomatic language encountered by students in their prescribed and recreational reading materials. Such information would be useful to educational authorities involved in the selection of school textbooks and in curricula planning. Aspiring authors of reading material designed for schools would no doubt also find the information useful.

The effect of idioms on types of reading material other than prose remains to be investigated. Perhaps the occurrence of idioms in the descriptive style of writing found in many social studies books would produce similar results.

Various methods of teaching an understanding of idioms should be explored. Should idioms be taught as isolated units, or should they be taught in context? Is it possible to train children to discern idioms by the use of context clues, or should idioms be taught through an understanding of metaphorical language? The answers to these and other questions would be instructive to teachers in the classroom.

The role of idioms in language may necessitate a modification of existing readability formulas to make allowance for a new level of difficulty in reading material, namely, the incidence and type of idiomatic expression encountered.

Reading selections of strictly literal material could serve as a transitional link between written Standard English and the multiplicity of dialects which exist in Canada today. This would, in effect, create three levels of English: nonliteral, literal, and dialect.

It is hoped that future research into reading difficulties experienced by Canadian children will concentrate more on the nonliteral aspects of English language. In this way, when there are valuable lessons to be learned from research studies in the United States of America and elsewhere, at least a comparative assessment will be possible.

references

1. Bolinger, Dwight. *Aspects of Language.* New York: Harcourt, Brace and World, 1968.
2. Chafe, Wallace L. "Idiomaticity as an Anomaly in the Chomskyan Paradigm," *Foundations of Language,* 1968, 4.
3. Chafe, Wallace L. "Language as Symbolization," *Language,* 1967, 43.
4. Dechant, Emerald V. *Improving the Teaching of Reading.* New Jersey: Prentice-Hall, 1970.
5. Lachenmeyer, Charles. "The Feeling of the Language of Literature: A Conceptual Analysis," *Linguistics.* Mouton: 1969, 55.
6. Makkai, Adam. "The Two Idiomaticity Areas in English and Their Membership: A Stratification View," *Linguistics.* Mouton: 1969, 50-53.
7. Pei, Mario, et al. *Language Today.* New York: Funk and Wagnalls, 1967.
8. Ruddell, Robert B. "Language Acquisition and the Reading Process," in Harry Singer and Robert Ruddell (Eds.), *Theoretical Models and Processes of Reading.* Newark, Delaware: International Reading Association, 1970.
9. Strickland, Ruth G. "The Language of Elementary School Children: Its Relationship to the Language of Reading Textbooks and the Quality of Reading of Selected Children," *Bulletin of the School of Education,* Indiana University, 1962, 38.
10. Wardhaugh, Ronald. "Current Linguistic Research and Its Implications for the Teaching of Reading," in J. Allen Figurel (Ed.), *Forging Ahead in Reading,* 1967 Proceedings, Volume 12, Part 1. Newark, Delaware: International Reading Association, 1968.
11. Winer, B. J. *Statistical Principles in Experimental Design.* Toronto: McGraw-Hill, 1971.

Peltz reports a study in which he repatterned the syntactical structure of eight social studies passages at the tenth grade level to determine the effect on the comprehension of thirty-four randomly selected tenth grade students. The study contributes some interesting insights about factors in the processes of reading and language as they affect the reader's performance.

using students' writing patterns to repattern reading material

fillmore k. peltz
springfield gardens, new york, high school

In this research, the investigator repatterned reading material by proportionally approximating the patterning found in an analysis of students' writing. This presentation will offer a brief description of the research, followed by an account of the procedures used in the language analysis and the repatterning. Final remarks will deal with insights derived from both findings and observations.

In this research, syntactic patterning was considered as an aspect of language which, when analyzed in terms of a psycholinguistic model of the reading process and a generative transformational grammar, might yield insights regarding the competence and performance of the reader.

the problem

The investigator assumed that patterning is a factor within both the linguistic expectations of the reader and the language production of the writer. This assumption grew out of two distinct theoretical constructs: 1) that reading is a psycholinguistic process in which the reader, an active language user, is influenced by personal linguistic expectations and experience, both of which have an effect upon his perception even before he begins the reading process (3); and 2) that language can be effectively described in terms of generative-transformational grammar which postulates that the writer's deep structure (concept) is generated into a surface structure (words, phrases, and clauses) as a consequence of the interaction and application of certain grammatical transformations (2).

Within this psycholinguistic framework, it seemed possible that the writer's linguistic expectations and experience influence his system of grammatical relations, the nature and extent of his lexicon, and his application of both necessary and optional grammatical transformations. Hence, it was postulated that the reader's approach to graphic, syntactic, and semantic perceptual input was a consequence of personal expectations and experience which could be markedly different from those of the writer. If this were the case, the expectations of the reader might be very difficult to reconcile with the structures generated by the writer.

purpose of the study

The specific purpose of this study was to determine the effect upon the average tenth grade learner's comprehension of repatterning representative passages from a tenth grade social studies text. Eight passages were repatterned to proportionally approximate the syntactic patterns found in a transformational analysis of the writing of the tenth grade subjects expected to read the text.

hypotheses

Three research hypotheses were tested. It was postulated that proportionally approximating the syntactic patterns of the written language of average tenth graders to repattern representative tenth grade reading material will have a positive effect upon tenth grade learners' comprehension as measured 1) by cloze test scored by exact word, 2) by cloze test scored by acceptable synonym and exact word, and 3) by multiple-choice test.

design of the study

Thus, the investigation necessitated a descriptive phase, in which both the writing of the tenth grade subjects and the representative passages were analyzed, and an experimental phase, in which the passages were repatterned and the subjects were tested on their comprehension of both the original and the repatterned versions.

The sample. The sample consisted of 34 students randomly selected from the tenth grade population of a large, integrated high school serving approximately 4,000 students in Queens, New York.

Instruments. The specific passages to be analyzed and repatterned were selected following the procedures outlined by Strickland (9). Insights derived from research by O'Donnell, Griffin, and Norris (8), Bateman and Zidonas (1), Mellon (7), and Hunt (4, 5, 6) were used to develop an analytic instrument designed to quantify the frequency with which 51 different transformations were generated both by the subjects and by the authors of the representative passages.

procedures

Collection and analysis of the writing sample. The subjects were asked to generate 1,000 words of prose which were then analyzed within the framework of a transformational grammar. The eight representative passages were subjected to identical analysis, and the resultant means then served as a basis for a syntactic comparison which demonstrated that the subjects' syntactic language patterns were significantly different from those of the authors of the representative passages.

The repatterned passages. The representative passages were then repatterned by proportionally approximating the frequency with which each of 51 different transformations would have been generated had the subjects written the passages. The repatterning was accomplished by eliminating transformations which exceeded, and incorporating transformations which fell short of, the frequency projected by the subjects' writing.

The comprehension tests. A cloze comprehension test was developed over each of the eight unaltered and the eight repatterned passages, and a multiple-choice test was constructed for each of passages two, four, six, and eight.

The research hypotheses—statistical analyses. The data collected during the comprehension testing were analyzed by separate, one-way analyses of variance tests in order to test the main effect, the form of the social studies passages (original versus repatterned).

findings

When measured by cloze tests scored by exact word, and exact word plus acceptable synonym, the subjects' comprehension test scores were significantly (.05) higher for the repatterned passages than for the original passages.

When measured by multiple-choice tests, the subjects' comprehension test scores on the repatterned passages were not significantly (.05) different from their scores on the original passages.

conclusions

The investigator concluded that:

1. A transformational analysis of the writing of learners and of content area materials which those same learners are expected to read, will probably yield syntactic patterns of written language which can be quantified and which demonstrate that the patterns generated by the learners are significantly different from those generated by the authors.

2. When measured by cloze tests, proportionally approximating the syntactic patterns of the written language generated by learners to repattern content area materials they are expected to read is likely to have a positive effect upon their comprehension. (When measured by multiple-choice test, proportionally approximating the learners' written syntactic language patterns did not appear to have a positive effect upon the comprehension of those same learners. This result may have been a consequence of the investigator's having constructed too difficult a multiple-choice test instrument, or it may underscore an area of considerable concern to current researchers, namely, whether multiple-choice and cloze tests measure the same comprehension factors.)

implications

The implications grow out of the demonstrated importance of both isolating and identifying those syntactic factors which contribute to the linguistic expectations of the reader and the language production of the writer. Consequently, the implications underscore the importance of incorporating a psycholinguistic model of the reading process into teaching, curriculum development, and textbook production as they appear to affect the language experience and expectations of the learner.

a description of the language analysis

Through a detailed analysis of the writing of the learners, the investigator attempted to isolate and identify those syntactic factors

Repatterning to Enhance Readability

which affect the language experience and expectations of the learner and which appear to warrant consideration when repatterning reading material.

Each of the writing samples was analyzed within the framework of a transformational grammar. First, the writing sample was divided into T-units. Then, every T-unit of each writing sample was analyzed (approximately 2,500 T-units), and the results of the total analysis were cast into 15 measures: the number of words, T-units, sentences, and clauses; the mean length of sentences, T-units, and clauses; the mean number of clauses per T-unit and of T-units per punctuated sentence; the number of instances, per 100 T-units, of the embedding of a nominal clause or phrase replacing a noun; the number of instances, per 100 T-units, of the expansion of a nominal by the addition of a relative clause, phrase, or word; and the number of instances, per 100 T-units, of embedding (items 10 through 14).

The findings regarding total number of words, T-units, sentences, and clauses were used to calculate a "synopsis of clause to sentence length factors." This synopsis consists of five ratios which yield the mean number of words per clause, clauses per T-unit, words per T-unit, T-units per sentence, and words per sentence.

synopsis of clause to sentence length factors

These five ratios were derived from the analysis of both the subjects' writing samples and the representative passages, and it was found that the mean number of words per sentence, per T-unit, and per clause were stochastically greater (.01) for the authors than for the subjects. The ratios also showed that the original passages utilized fewer subordinate clauses and fewer instances of main clause coordination. Since the authors of the social studies passages actually used fewer clauses, the addition of clausal structures could not account for the longer sentences and T-units generated. The length of these structures, then, was apparently a result of factors within clauses. Hence, it appeared necessary to seek within each clause in order to isolate factors which might be used in repatterning. Five additional measures were calculated in order to determine the number and type of embedding transformations generated within each clause.

embedding transformations

Thirty-four different types of embedding transformations were analyzed. Fifteen of these transformations were at the clausal level and served to provide greater specificity regarding the ratio reflecting the number of subordinate clauses used per T-unit; the remaining nineteen embedding transformations were at the phrase and word levels. They were designed to analyze and record the number and type of embedding transformations used to replace or expand nominal structures within each clause. At the phrase level, the investigator recorded the frequency with which seven different transformations were used to replace a noun or pronoun with a nominal phrase. For example, in the sentence *It is exciting* the infinitive phrase *to appear on television* may be optionally generated and used to replace the pronoun *it* resulting in the sentence *To appear on television is exciting.* Such a structure was considered an example of the use of a replacement transformation. At both the phrase and the word levels, the frequency with which twelve different transformations were used to expand (modify) a noun were recorded. (In these instances, the relative phrases and words were interpreted to be kernel sentences transformed to relative clauses and then optionally reduced to phrases or single words. For example, the clause *who is on the field* is reduced to the phrase *on the field* in the sentence *The boy on the field scored yesterday.* The clause *who is handsome* is reduced to the single word *handsome* in the sentence *The handsome boy laughed.* In such instances, the writer was considered to have employed an optional expansion transformation which embeds a kernel sentence.)

embedding transformations—findings

As a result of the analysis of embedding transformations, it was found that at the clausal level the authors embedded both fewer nominal and fewer relative (adjective) clauses than did the subjects. The authors' clauses were longer as a result of the fact that, at the phrase level, they embedded more than twice the number of kernel sentences using nominal phrases to replace nouns. When expanding (modifying) a noun, the authors generated almost four times the number of relative phrases and more than twice the number of relative words.

In summary, each time a subject embedded a single kernel sentence within a T-unit (added a concept to an existing structure), the authors of the social studies passages embedded between three and four kernel sentences.

the repatterning procedure

Therefore, the investigator repatterned the original passages by proportionally approximating the frequency with which each of 51 different types of transformations would have been generated had the subjects written the passages. First, the number of T-units in the representative passages was adjusted to reflect the number of T-units which the subjects would have generated had they written an equivalent number of words. The adjusted figure was arrived at by dividing the total number of words in the representative passages by the mean number of words per T-unit generated by the subjects. Then, the projected frequency of each transformation was calculated by computing the following ratio:

$$\frac{\text{Adjusted total number of T-units}}{\text{Total number of T-units in the subjects' essays}} = \frac{\text{Projected frequency}}{\text{Frequency with which the transformation was generated per 100 T-units in the subjects' essays}}$$

Repeated computations of this ratio projected a proportional approximation of the frequency with which the subjects would have used each embedding transformation had they written the 2,074 words which comprised the original passages. (The repatterning was executed over all eight passages.) Guided by the projected frequency of use of each embedding transformation, the investigator developed the repatterned passages by eliminating transformations which exceeded and by incorporating transformations which fell short of the frequency projected for the subjects. It was the investigator's belief that truly deleting phrases and words would, as a necessary consequence, reduce the level of vocabulary difficulty, thereby confounding the results of the study. Consequently, in most instances, the words and phrases which had been embedded in nominal structures were "eliminated" in that they were changed, through the use of optional transformations, into active verbs and adverbial structures.

the repatterned passages—analysis and findings

When the repatterning was completed, the repatterned passages were analyzed in terms of the mean measures into which the analysis of the subjects' essays had been cast and were compared to the subjects' essays in terms of both the synopsis of clause to sentence length factors and the total number of embedding transformations per 100 T-units.

The mean number of words per clause and per sentence calculated for the repatterned passages were not significantly (.05) different from the mean number calculated for the subjects' essays. There was no significant (.05) difference in the use of either subordinate or co-ordinate constructions. Only the mean number of words per T-unit was stochastically greater (.05) for the repatterned passages than for the subjects' essays. This last finding may have been a result of the fact that, in order to preserve vocabulary difficulty, words and phrases which were used to replace or expand nominal structures with a frequency which exceeded that demonstrated by the subjects, were not deleted but were retransformed into active verbs and adverbial forms. Lastly, the total mean number of embedding transformations generated per 100 T-units by the subjects was not significantly (.05) different from the total mean number of embedding transformations used in the repatterned passages. Thus, it appears that repatterning based upon the quantification of specific syntactic factors is a promising procedure.

Two remaining observations seem to reinforce this premise. The investigator compared the findings of Hunt's study (4) *Grammatical Structures Written at Three Grade Levels,* with those for the authors of the social studies passages used in the present investigation. In his study, Hunt analyzed the writing of subjects at three grade levels (four, eight, and twelve) and of "superior" adults writing for *Harper's* and *Atlantic.* A comparison of the findings reveals that the authors of the social studies passages generated almost an identical mean number of words per clause as did Hunt's "superior" adults, but that the mean number of clauses per T-unit of the authors most closely approaches that calculated for Hunt's eighth grade subjects. In addition, while the mean number of T-units per sentence generated by both the present tenth grade subjects and the authors was not significantly different, the mean calculated for the latter did not fall between twelfth graders and "superior" adults as might have been expected.

Thus, the authors may have utilized syntactic patterning which diverged considerably from what Hunt appears to have demonstrated to be a developmental balance of underlying syntactic factors contributing to sentence length. The synopsis of clause to sentence length factors of the language production of authors writing a tenth grade social studies text was not consistent with what might have been either projected for tenth graders or expected for "superior" adults who, in this case, were the authors themselves.

repatterning in order to enhance readability

The foregoing is particularly noteworthy when we consider that the authors of the social studies passages, writing for the average reader in a nation-wide market, were apparently concerned with making their text as readable as possible and were also aware of the readability criteria of vocabulary difficulty and sentence length. This very awareness may have had an effect upon their language production. The authors may have attempted to improve readability by generating sentences which were consistent with the established criterion of sentence length, but which were, nonetheless, inconsistent with the subjects' experiences and expectations. The sentence length generated by the authors approached that length which is consistent with the readability expectations for grade ten; however, the criterion of sentence length was realized through the generation of relatively few subordinate and coordinate constructions, thus offsetting the factor contributed by a clause length consistent with the linguistic expectations of the readers of *Harper's* and *Atlantic.*

Finally, while the investigator attempted to limit the current research to syntactic considerations, one observation bearing on a semantic element is that the authors used many more hyphenated words than did the subjects: hunter-farmer, village-farming, flat-topped, best-known, well-built, well-planted, one-room, low-grade, good-grade, fifty-year, age-old. It is interesting that while the authors may have attempted to improve readability by generating semantic structures which may be classed as familiar vocabulary in readability analyses, when approached within the framework of a transformational grammar, they may represent structures which are inconsistent with the expectation and experience of the intended readers. Each structure embeds at least two concepts, and in the case of *hunter-farmer,* there are no fewer than four separate concepts.

Thus, repatterning textual material in a content area in terms of the current criteria of vocabulary difficulty and sentence length may result in the creation of an artificial language that is both syntactically and semantically different from the linguistic expectations and experiences of the learner. Attempts to manipulate sentence length may ignore intrasentence factors which significantly contribute to sentence length. Attempts to simplify vocabulary may result in the creation of structures which, while they are composed of "familiar" words, inadvertently embed concepts in a manner which may, therefore, result in semantic structures and a conceptual load which are out of the learner's realm of expectation and experience.

The foregoing does not propose that the current criteria of sentence length and vocabulary difficulty are not effective indices with which to measure language that is naturally produced. It is rather the reversal of the process, the utilization of these indices in order to restructure language which is then measured by those very same indices, which is here called into serious question.

Therefore, this investigator urges that any process designed to restructure language should incorporate the insights of both the psycholinguistic model of the reading process and generative-transformational grammar.

references

1. Bateman, Donald, and Frank Zidonas. *The Effect of a Study of Transformational Grammar on the Writing of Ninth and Tenth Graders,* Research Report No. 6. Champaign, Illinois: National Council of Teachers of English, 1966.
2. Chomsky, Noam. *Aspects of the Theory of Syntax.* Cambridge: Massachusetts Institute of Technology Press, 1965.
3. Goodman, Kenneth S. "Reading: A Psycholinguistic Guessing Game, in Harry Singer and Robert B. Ruddell (Eds.), *Theoretical Models and Processes of Reading.* Newark, Delaware: International Reading Association, 1970.
4. Hunt, Kellogg W. *Grammatical Structures Written at Three Grade Levels,* Research Report No. 3. Champaign, Illinois: National Council of Teachers of English, 1965.
5. Hunt, Kellogg W. *Sentence Structures Used by Superior Students in Grades Four and Twelve, and by Superior Adults.* Washington, D.C.: U.S. Department of Health, Education, and Welfare. (Microfiche ED 010 047)
6. Hunt, Kellogg W. *Syntactic Maturity in School Children and Adults,* Monographs of the Society for Research in Child Development, 35, No. 1. Chicago: University of Chicago Press, 1970.
7. Mellon, John C. *Transformational Sentence-Combining,* Research Report No. 10. Champaign, Illinois: National Council of Teachers of English, 1969.
8. O'Donnell, Roy C., William J. Griffin, and Raymond C. Norris. *Syntax of Kindergarten and Elementary School Children: A Transformational Analysis,* Research Report No. 8. Champaign, Illinois: National Council of Teachers of English, 1967.
9. Strickland, Ruth G. *The Language of Elementary School Children: Its Relationship to the Language of Reading Textbooks and the Quality of Reading of Selected Children.* Bloomington: Indiana University, School of Education, 1962.

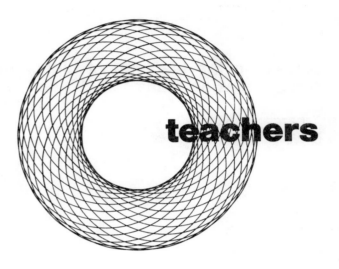

teachers

The teacher's role in reading instruction is of paramount importance. Smith asks nine questions of teachers to focus attention on evaluation of teacher roles in developing higher level comprehension skills.

evaluating the teaching of higher level comprehension skills

richard j. smith
university of wisconsin

The ultimate objective of reading instruction is to provide students with the necessary skills and attitudes for using print to enrich their lives. Reading instruction is a failure when it falls short of this goal. Print is a symbol system and Moffett (3) says, "Symbol systems are not primarily about themselves; they are about other subjects. When a student 'learns' one of these systems, he 'learns how' to operate it. The main point is to think and talk about other things by means of this system."

Observation of instructional reading programs indicates that the reading experiences some students have in school are more mechanical than meaningful and are more productive of correct responses to factual recall questions and multiple-choice items than productive of satisfaction from sharing ideas with an author. Short selections from basal readers or kits are read, the accompanying comprehension checks are done immediately and quickly, and the selection is promptly forgotten. Students are moved through a progression of short selections and related exercises that often only faintly resemble the communication process that reading should be. The selections and exercises, however, do resemble the tasks students are asked to perform on standardized reading achievement tests. Consequently, students may be evaluated as superior readers when in fact they are relatively immature readers in regard to their abilities to use reading to solve problems, apply ideas read about in one content area to another, detect an author's bias, evaluate their own biases, see themselves in a literary character, or arrive at a new idea not directly expressed by the author.

Principals and other instructional leaders need to employ some guidelines that go beyond the findings of standardized tests to ascertain whether higher level comprehension abilities are being developed as part of the reading program. The content of the materials, the instructional practices of the teachers, and the reading related activities of the students must be carefully examined. Reading programs need balance, and one dimension of a balanced reading program is thought that involves analytic, creative, critical, and other higher level cognitive behaviors related to reading selections. The following questions are meant to be helpful to principals in purchasing materials, supervising teachers, and evaluating the effects of the reading program in this regard.

1. *Is the content of the reading material well written and relevant to the student with whom it is used?*

There is no substitute for good material. Interesting characters, vivid descriptions, and unified and coherent paragraphs permit students to empathize, visualize, and think through an idea with an author. The producers of some developmental materials have devised elaborate word attack cues, comprehension questions, work sheets, and other instructional aids for material that is poorly written and/or not relevant to the experiences and interests of the students for whom it is intended. Attractive packaging sometimes hides dull, meaningless material that students merely repeat or read to answer simple questions. The development of higher level comprehension skills begins with good narrative or expository writing.

2. *Are teachers asking questions that require higher level thinking?*

A number of classroom interaction studies have shown a striking avoidance of the kinds of questions that elicit thinking above the memory level. Questions asked before and after reading can direct students to make applications, see relationships, and read beyond the lines of print. Sanders' book, *Classroom Questions: What Kinds?* (4), has been useful in helping teachers construct questions at the higher cognitive levels.

When a teacher does not ask a question that requires higher level thinking, the students may raise their hands to answer before the teacher finishes asking the question. Students who "jump the gun" have apparently learned to expect questions that can be answered without much thinking.

3. *Are teachers providing the thinking time necessary for students to answer questions above the cognitive level of memory?*

The classroom is a busy place with schedules to be maintained and work to be done. It is not uncommon for a teacher to ask a thought-provoking question, become increasingly uncomfortable as precious seconds are filled with silence, interrupt student thinking with more cues to the desired response, and, just as students are beginning to put things together in their minds, supply the answer to the question. Teachers should encourage verbalization and overt activity in their classrooms, but the kind of thinking necessary for developing higher level comprehension skills often demands student reflection which the teacher should not perceive as wasteful.

4. *What kinds of activities are teachers involving students in relative to their reading?*

Teachers can teach students to look for relationships, evaluate ideas, create new ideas or products and engage in other mature reading behaviors by involving students in activities related to reading selections. A good story might give rise to a simulated author-meets-the-critics interview, a mock trial of the main character, or the creation of a new character or bit of dialogue to interject at some point in the story. An account of some historical happening read in a textbook might lead to a student debate, a written newspaper account of the event, or posters designed to portray the event. Choral reading of certain poems or writing plays to dramatize a particular period in the life of a great scientist who was discussed in a reading selection are other ways of helping students see the possibilities for stretching their minds while reading. Teachers who cannot, or who do not, take the time and expend the energy to get students to respond to reading in interesting, meaningful activities are missing opportunities to teach higher level comprehension skills.

5. *Are teachers providing the experiential background necessary for gaining a full understanding of reading selections?*

What a reader takes away from a reading selection depends to a large extent upon what he brings to it. Seeing implications and detecting subtleties, irony, or cynicism in a reading selection all require some experiential commonalities between the author and the reader. A major cause of poor comprehension is that the author and the reader are playing in different ballparks. As Professor Harold Hill proved in *The Music Man,* "You gotta know the territory."

6. *Are teachers giving prereading instruction that directs students to employ higher level comprehension skills while reading?*

Students will read for the purposes that are set for them. If, before they begin, they are told to watch for propaganda techniques or implications for changing their lifestyles, students will read for those purposes. No successful coach sends the team on to the field of play without a game plan. Yet many teachers wait until after the reading is completed to let students know what great opportunities the selection held for mature thinking experiences.

7. *Are teachers "readers" in the best sense of the word?*

Johnson *(2)* says, "Reading is something we do, not so much with our eyes, as such, as with our knowledge and interests and enthusiasm, our hatred and fondnesses and fears, our evaluations in all their forms and aspects. Because this is so, a fondness for reading is something that a child acquires in much the same way as he catches a cold —by being effectively exposed to someone who already has it." Teachers who are themselves infrequent or superficial readers may pass their limited concepts of reading on to their students. Gans *(1)* says, "When I go into a group, I realize first of all that I carry something in. I reflect what I think reading means." Principals who want their students to develop and use higher level comprehension skills should hire teachers who have developed and who use higher level comprehension skills. One aspect of a good interview or conference would be to ask prospective or practicing teachers to discuss something they are reading currently or have read recently.

8. *Are students given opportunities to read some self-selected material and converse with other students about it?*

Higher level comprehension skills are more likely to be employed when students are reading material that interests them. Free reading time should be allocated at all grade levels as a major dimension of the school reading program. Unless school time is provided, the students who need reading practice most will get the least. Practice reading is essential for interpretive, critical, creative, and other higher level thinking behaviors to become an integral part of a student's reading performance. It is also important to have opportunities to converse about reading experiences with other students in small groups without a lot of structure or focus. During these informal discussions students learn what other students get from their reading and, by verbalizing their own reactions to a reading selection they become more keenly aware of the mental processes employed while reading. One student remarked, "It's when I talk about it that I really understand it."

RICHARD J. SMITH

9. *Are students using reading to satisfy their informational and recreational needs?*

Students who are not learning to use higher level comprehension skills are likely to find severe limitations in the power of reading to satisfy their personal needs. Students who cannot comprehend beyond the level of literal interpretation will probably turn to sources other than reading to solve their problems. A well-balanced reading program stimulates students to read books, magazines, and newspapers; to ask for books; to use the library; and to talk about what they read. Students who like reading (meaning reading instruction) but who don't read are products of a reading program which leads nowhere.

references

1. Gans, Roma. "Meeting the Challenges of the Middle Grades," *What Is Reading Doing to the Child?* Highlights from the Sixteenth Annual Reading Conference of Lehigh University. Danville, Illinois: Interstate Printers, 1967.

2. Johnson, Wendell. *Your Most Enchanted Listener.* New York: Harper & Row, 1956, 123.

3. Moffett, James. *Teaching the Universe of Discourse.* Boston: Houghton Mifflin, 1968, 6.

4. Sanders, Norris M. *Classroom Questions: What Kinds?* New York: Harper & Row, 1966.

Providing the necessary inservice training in teaching reading for content teachers is a task to which we must direct persistent efforts if we are to produce better readers at all levels. "Operation READS" gives us one approach for accomplishing this worthy goal.

every teacher a teacher of reading— for only a week

dan dramer
central high school
franklin square, new york

How often have you heard "Every teacher is a teacher of reading"? In secondary schools, reading teachers are the only ones who believe this hackneyed statement. Subject teachers can't be blamed for wanting to duck the responsibility of teaching reading. A chemistry teacher didn't sweat through inorganic and organic chemistry and qualitative and quantitative analysis only to wind up teaching the short a sound. Of course, science teachers do want their pupils to be able to read well, but they don't want to be the persons who teach reading, and they don't want reading time to impinge on their subject content time.

Reading teachers argue that only a content teacher can teach the vocabulary of his own subject, and that those vocabulary words are most meaningful when taught at the appropriate time in the subject classroom to which they apply. Reading teachers quote good, solid research to show that when reading is taught during "regular" subject area time in a content classroom, not only do pupils learn to read better, they also achieve better in the subject content. Reading teachers cite studies which they believe demonstrate beyond doubt that reading skills and subject content can be taught simultaneously by the content teacher and with advantages to both. We cite, we quote, we demonstrate—but to little avail. Math teachers are not reading teachers; by temperament, by training, and by title, they are math teachers and math is what they intend to go on teaching. They want their pupils to have reading, but they want reading teachers to do the teaching.

overview of one solution

Operation READS, Sewanhaka Central High School District's program of reading in the content areas, has really made every teacher a teacher of reading. The secret lies in limiting the program to one week. Happily, it has become a full-time activity for many teachers.

Operation READS is an all-out mobilization of all the resources of our secondary school district of twelve-thousand pupils on a concentration in reading. Every pupil in grades seven through nine participates in nearly every subject: art, English, home economics, mathematics, physical education, science, and social studies. For example, for five school days, every pupil takes how-to-read math instead of regular math or how-to-read science in place of regular science. He is taught by his regular math and science teachers who truly become teachers of reading—if only for a week.

How have we convinced content teachers that they do indeed have a responsibility for teaching reading? Five important program components insure success: 1) development of well-written and worthwhile reading materials based on topics which the teachers normally would teach at that particular period of the school day; 2) delimitation of reading-teaching involvement to a single, obviously relevant, easily explained, specific study skill; 3) careful inservice orientation; 4) a publicity campaign which includes appeals from the administration; and 5) feedback and evaluation.

selecting the topic

The district reading supervisor met extensively with department chairmen. Corporately, they suggested a unit of study for each subject which would be compatible with the curriculum for the school year. The teaching units were developed by a content area teacher with the assistance of reading specialists.

delimiting the reading involvement

The only reading-study skill involved was the Survey Q3R Study Method (1). Pupils used the Survey Q3R method on the normal textbook units pertaining to the area covered.

Teachers experienced in each of the subjects, selected for their writing ability, were paid to author special materials during two weeks of the summer vacation. Two reading specialists provided two initial days of basic reading instruction and stayed with the project to provide the reading expertise. The materials were mimeographed in workbook form, applying SQ3R to the actual textbooks the pupils used during the program. Extensive teacher manuals were provided. Some idea of the scope of the project may be gained from the fact that 300,000 pages, many of them consumable, were mimeographed that summer.

inservice orientation

It was necessary to convince subject teachers, unenthusiastic about the prospect of teaching reading, that the SQ3R was an effective study method by having them actually experience its efficacy through personal involvement. The assembled teachers were allowed four minutes to skim a selected chapter in a Canadian history text, chosen because it was nontechnical and an unfamiliar subject to most teachers. Since four minutes' time was not enough for even fast readers to complete the chapter, and since most of the teachers had little skill in skimming or studying, the group wound up with a mark of 20 percent on the end-of-chapter test—a mark that chance alone would have provided. The reading supervisor then presented the five-step SQ3R study method. At the conclusion of the presentation, the teacher group was led over a four minute survey of another chapter selected from the Canadian history. With no further reading, they achieved 80 percent as a class average on the end-of-chapter test. They had proved for themselves that SQ3R works.

After learning basic SQ3R, teachers of one subject met in small groups with reading specialists and with the subject teachers who had, over the summer, written the materials to be used in the program. The teachers left these meetings "sold," but it was still necessary to convince their pupils.

publicity campaign

Operation READS (Reading Embracing All Disciplines at Sewanhaka) was launched with all the ballyhoo the district was capable of mustering. A month before the start of the program, each school's walls were papered with posters cryptically proclaiming, "Operation READS is coming." Then, each week for a month, additional posters provided further details until the entire program had been sketched in. The chief administrator and building principals took to closed-circuit TV and to their public address systems to plug Operation READS.

the program in action

During the week of the actual program, reading truly became *the* school effort. Pupils were bombarded with SQ3R in each of their subjects. Administrators and reading specialists walked the corridors to lend support and to secure additional materials if necessary.

Pupils were totally immersed in reading. Even in art (previously regarded as a purely manipulative subject), students were SQ3Ring their way through reading materials in history of architecture. All subject area teachers had truly become teachers of reading.

feedback and evaluation

Many instruments were used to evaluate the project. Scales were devised to help classroom teachers rate their classes on knowledge of study method and/or ability to apply study skills to content material. All kinds of performance-referenced criteria were provided in a thirty-page evaluation packet. The general results indicated that, before participating in Operation READS and despite good teaching in the elementary grades, pupils had entered secondary school without any real knowledge of a system for studying. By the end of the program, students had been exposed in depth to the SQ3R method and they had had a chance to apply it, both under teacher direction and on their own, to a wide variety of materials in different subjects. Although some pupils may have been taught SQ3R till they winced at the letters, our evaluations demonstrated that pupils learned and used SQ3R.

The teachers' anonymous questionnaires were collated, analyzed, and published, subject-by-subject and school-by-school—a practice continued for the five years Operation READS was in effect. One item on the questionnaires gave teachers five alternatives—five votes to determine the future of the program. The five choices ranged from, "Next year the program should be summarily dropped" to "Next year the program should be extended in length and moved up to include the next higher grade level." On the basis of questionnaire results, the program was moved from grade seven, where it originated, to include grades seven through nine.

The one-week length of the program is believed to be its great strength. Even the most subject-oriented teacher can be persuaded to devote one week to reading. And for that one week teachers and administrators can maintain an all-out effort to teach reading skills.

Operation READS has convinced a lot of subject area teachers that they are responsible for teaching reading in their classrooms. It has taught them a method and provided them with a vehicle for accomplishing the teaching of reading. Operation READS has proved that all teachers are, indeed, teachers of reading—if only for a week.

reference

1. Robinson, Francis P. *Effective Study.* New York: Harper Brothers, 1946.

Although this paper addresses the issue of inservice training for teachers of minority students, it also provides ideas applicable to any inservice program.

classroom teacher + reading consultant = successful inservice education

marian a. wright
pueblo high school
tucson, arizona

Content area teachers in today's urban schools may have Indian, Mexican-American, Black, Chinese, and Anglo students enrolled in the same class. Recognizing the cultural and ability range existing in any one class presents an awesome challenge that can perhaps be successfully met by combining the talents of the classroom teacher with those of the reading consultant.

The reading consultant should be able to: conduct inservice workshops in reading in the content areas; present methods of individualized instruction applicable to the Indian, Mexican-American, and other minority students who have limited English language backgrounds; demonstrate teaching of effective ways of including reading skills in the content areas; develop lesson plans incorporating levels of comprehension to meet the wide range of abilities usually found in any one classroom; assist discouraged students; locate and provide suitable materials; conduct diagnostic testing; teach reading skills needed for effective use of the school library; lead in team teaching; and, perhaps most important of all, develop a sensitivity to teacher needs and the best ways to meet them.

"Developing a total-school approach to the reading instruction in senior high schools is still a pioneering enterprise. Two factors cause this approach to be especially difficult: 1) the teachers who are asked to play major roles in the instructional reading program are often not convinced that this is a legitimate responsibility for them to assume, and 2) secondary school teachers are generally untrained in reading theory and methodology for teaching reading in the content areas" (2). High schools that find it possible to initiate the program through an inservice workshop will pave the way for acceptance and understanding of the program.

Several high school administrators and department chairmen, determined to place more emphasis on reading in the content areas, asked the authors to direct an inservice workshop in "Reading in the Content Areas" the week before school officially opened. Teachers who enrolled received two hours of credit on the salary scale. These faculty members would serve as a nucleus to encourage other members of the faculty to recognize the need for including reading skills in their content areas. Departments represented were Home Economics, Foreign Languages, English, Business Education, Science, and Industrial Arts.

The workship assignment was to prepare materials for the first two weeks of the school term and incorporate in those materials specific reading skills. Materials to be used the first week were diagnostic in nature and were to furnish each teacher with clues concerning the reading levels of every student enrolled in class. For the second week, participants prepared their regular class materials, but they incorporated specific reading skills.

The workshop director demonstrated the above techniques as they might apply to an English class. The teachers, in a role-playing situation, filled out a Reading Diagnostic Record for High School and College Students (3). Various interest inventories were presented and discussed. A lesson plan was presented using the school newspaper to teach skimming and fact-finding. Vocabulary and spelling techniques were demonstrated. Supplementary help, available to all teachers, was reviewed (student folders, for example, yield valuable information about past reading performance and health problems such as vision or hearing; nurses can supply help with student health problems; and counsellors and reading consultant services can help determine a student's current reading level.

Each teacher in the group was given independent study time to prepare similar diagnostic materials adapted to their particular content areas. The workshop director served as a resource person and was available for consultation during the independent study time. It should be stressed here that workshops be structured so that teachers prepare concrete materials which can be used in their classrooms. Since no one method is effective for all, it is important for teachers to be allowed to weave new ideas into their own style of teaching.

Each member of the workshop demonstrated one diagnostic lesson for the class. An English teacher demonstrated levels of comprehension as applied to a short story she planned to teach. Her lesson plan followed the literal, interpretive, and applied levels of comprehension as developed by Herber (1): "The literal level of comprehension applied to a content textbook produces knowledge of what the author said in order to derive meaning from his statement. . . . The applied level of comprehension takes the product of the literal, what the author has said, and the interpretive, what the author meant by what he said, and applies it in some pragmatic or theoretical exercise." Analysis of student answers to questions designed to test all three levels would give insight concerning each student's level of comprehension. The teacher also would use student answers to diagnose mastery of sentence structure, spelling, and vocabulary range.

The industrial arts instructor used an auto mechanics text, high school reading level, to demonstrate the Survey Q3R technique he would use to introduce the text to his auto mechanics class: "The *survey* involves preliminary thinking about the chapter or article. What is my purpose in reading it? What do I already know about it? If I were the author, what would I say about the subject?" Also included is a skimming of the material to orient the reader and give him the opportunity to decide on the reading method to use. Q refers to questions that might be answered by the selection. These are questions to which the reader wants the answer or questions which a rapid skimming shows can be answered in the selection. The second R stands for review to check one's comprehension of the selection. The third R suggests that the student recite what was gained from the reading in the form in which it will probably be used (4).

One home economics teacher devised a lesson to test student mastery of the vocabulary needed to read recipe directions. A teacher of ESL (English as a second language), who would be teaching Indian and Mexican-American students with limited English facility, developed an interest inventory in English and Spanish that would provide her with clues to student abilities and interests: Is the student truly bilingual? Can the student read and write in both languages, or can he read and write only in his native language? Does the student only

70

speak his native language without being able to read and write it? What interest does he have that can be utilized to motivate his learning?

A readability index was used by the science teacher to determine the reading level of the various science texts he planned to use. After determining the approximate grade level of the vocabulary and sentence structure, he wrote a brief diagnostic test using four increasingly difficult paragraphs taken from the science texts he would be using. Each paragraph was followed by three questions including the literal, applied, and interpretive level.

The new text to be used in the Spanish classes was surveyed by the class under the direction of the Spanish teacher. Business teachers developed an outline for a chapter in an exploratory business class.

Teacher reactions to the workshop were positive for several reasons: the workshop combined instruction, demonstration, independent study, involvement, and increased teacher awareness of responsibility for including reading skills in the content areas. Further, each teacher was free to incorporate needed reading skills into the material utilized for each class. However, through diagnostic teaching the teacher became aware of student capacity for mastering individual class materials. Each teacher included techniques designed to assure some success for all students. Each member reported the acquisition of valuable insights into the total school program through the presentations by the different departments.

One month into the school term, conferences were held with each member of the workshop to evaluate the results of the diagnostic materials developed and used during the opening weeks of school. English teachers, enthusiastic about the paragraphs and questions they had developed for diagnostic purposes, shared them with all teachers in their department; other workshop members demonstrated lessons they had developed on levels of comprehension.

Faculty acceptance of the reading consultant's role in the total school program can be improved through an inservice workshop; however, with or without a workshop, reading consultants must prove their usefulness in order to be accepted by teachers who already face a crowded schedule. The reading consultant's first ally should be the principal. Department chairmen can be encouraged by the principal to invite the consultant to department meetings to explain the program and the consultant should be prepared to demonstrate some techniques which could be shared with teachers in their content field.

Content area teachers are often not aware of the many reading skills they already teach. A dramatic way to begin the meeting is to hand each faculty member a list of the 99 reading skills listed by Herber (1). Each teacher should be asked to quickly check only those skills that would be inherent in their content area. The list includes skills found in every content area; for example, vocabulary, use of graphs and diagrams, following directions, interpretations, inferences, conclusions, and point of view. Teachers, of course, soon discover they are checking nearly every skill on the list! Which areas cause the most difficulty? In schools with high proportions of minority children teachers may answer with "The English vocabulary is too difficult," "The students don't find the material relevant," "Some of the students tune me out," "Some students talk all the time," "Some students won't respond at all," "We tried using the library, but some of the students couldn't find their books," or "Students who are absent get behind and there isn't time to help them catch up."

The consultant can respond to each problem mentioned with an offer that may help teachers find their own solutions. If students find the vocabulary too difficult, offer to develop a lesson that teaches the vocabulary in context. If asked to demonstrate the lesson, agree to do so. If the teacher just wants the lesson plan, write it.

Offer to locate suitable materials that will be relevant to the students. Develop a lesson plan using the school newspaper to teach skimming and fact finding skills. Most students like to read about their own school activities. If you suspect students of behavior problems because the material is too difficult, suggest other materials. If the class, for whatever reason, is required to use the same text, offer to demonstrate the Survey Q3R technique explained earlier in this article. An excellent way to get acquainted with all freshman students and their English teachers is to design a unit for teaching effective use of the school library. Most high schools have sophisticated libraries stocked with excellent supplementary books, magazines, reference aids, and filmstrips; but beginning high school students lack the skills to use these valuable aids effectively. Do not assume that students understand the card files, the Dewey Decimal system, or the location and availability of books and magazines. Develop simple lessons that can be taught through the combined talents of the classroom teacher, the librarian, and the reading consultant. Accompany each freshman English class to the library once a week for five or six weeks until the students have demonstrated mastery of the card files, reference materials, nonfiction, and fiction selections. Some teachers also will ask you to teach the use of *The Reader's Guide to Periodical Literature.*

Teachers may request your help with certain students who fall behind the class or just give up. It is hoped you will be allowed to assist the students in the regular classroom during study periods. This approach is more successful than one in which students are taken out of assigned classes to work wherever a vacant spot can be found. If teachers want individual testing or more insight into the reasons why a student is experiencing difficulty, the consultant should offer to check the student's folder and consult with his counselor and school nurse. This check may reveal situations such as the following: students who have "lost" or "broken" their glasses, students who are too shy or withdrawn to admit they don't understand, students who would function better in another class where emphasis is placed on skills they lack, and students who need tutoring for brief periods to get back on schedule.

If consultants develop sensitivity to teacher needs and offer ways of meeting those needs, they will be accepted as valuable additions to the total school program. And students of all ethnic groups will be the winners.

references

1. Herber, Harold L. *Teaching Reading in the Content Areas.* Englewood Cliffs, New Jersey: Prentice-Hall, 1970, 61-101.
2. Smith, Richard. "Developing a Total School Reading Program in a Senior High School," in B. Fallon and D. Filgro (Eds.), *Forty States Innovate to Improve School Reading Programs.* Bloomington, Indiana: Phi Delta Kappa, 1970, 140.
3. Strang, Ruth, et al. *Reading Diagnostic Record for High School and College Students.* New York: Bureau of Publications, Teachers College, Columbia University, 1952.
4. Strang, Ruth. *The Improvement of Reading* (3rd ed.). New York: McGraw-Hill, 1961, 389-390.

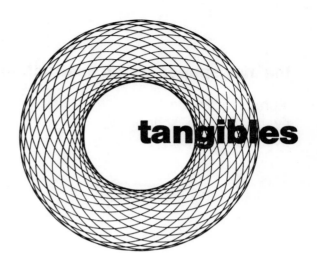

tangibles

The newspaper functions as an excellent teaching resource for reading instruction. Johnson cites many values of using the newspaper in the classroom.

the newspaper as an instructional medium

laura s. johnson
evanston high school
evanston, illinois

The pinch engendered by inflation and falling tax revenue puts many school administrators and faculty into a seemingly impossible bind when it comes to supplying their students with current yet academically acceptable reading materials. The newspaper, however, costs only a few cents per day per copy (each teacher can use one set of papers all day for all students). In addition, the newspaper provides many fringe benefits for both teachers and students.

The International Reading Association, with its worldwide membership of more than 55,000 professionals, encourages use of the newspaper (2):

> The newspaper is the most widely and consistently read piece of literature published. It should, therefore, have a prominent place in the school curriculum. Much can be taught from the newspaper because it contains much. Besides material for teaching reading skills, there are arithmetic problems, science information, historical events, entertainment features, and a panorama of societal needs and challenges.

Education U.S.A. (4) emphasizes the importance of newspapers in this way:

Students who use newspapers in the classroom become more understanding and analytical newspaper readers than those who don't, according to the results of a test designed by Educational Testing Service of Princeton, N. J. . . . . Comprehension of various sections of the newspaper was significantly higher in classes that had used newspapers.

The Newspaper in the Classroom Program has gained a great deal of acceptance in the past five years as more and more schools adopt it for prolonged as well as short-term use. Consider the following rate of growth between the 1966-1967 and the 1970-1971 school years: In the United States and Canada the number of students using newspapers in their classrooms increased 63 percent, the number of schools using newspapers increased 53 percent, and the number of teachers using newspapers increased 51 percent (1).

When academic personnel are in the process of considering widespread adoption of the newspaper for use in their classrooms, they want answers to two important questions: 1) How can an inexpensive, transitory item like a newspaper establish itself as acceptable classroom reading? and 2) Why, until recently, has the newspaper been so little used in schools?

To answer the first question: Newspapers are valuable in the classroom for many reasons. One is that the daily newspaper offers a viable, up-to-the-minute printout for keeping any textbook current. The time lag for publishing and distributing an author's book manuscript is usually one year; more often the lag is two or three years. A good teacher keeps the textbook current by supplementing the content with new information which has been printed since the book was copyrighted (5). This supplementing must be a constantly recurring process rather than just an occasional one. Although teachers are pressed for time to cover traditionally required work (and, if something has to go, it will be the newspaper rather than the textbook), responsibility to students requires teachers to use both the textbook and the newspaper.

Current print should be checked daily. This is important, not only for keeping subject matter up-to-date, but also for giving the student endless opportunities to practice restructuring what he already knows in terms of what the new item of information does to change the significance of older items. This is a student's real reason for being in school; he needs the creative experience of combining old and new so that he can produce an extended meaning. If the student does not have a chance to work with all of the materials which enable him to have this creative experience, he is being deprived of the most basic elements of education. He needs both the textbook and the daily printout to complete and integrate his process of education.

When the student reads like this, he is employing reading as a thought process in a manner which will vastly improve his ability to remember, to comprehend, and to synthesize. Let us turn to biology for an example of the importance of combining textbook and newspaper. What the book has to say about the cell is fundamental knowledge which the student must possess if he is to understand further information he reads or hears about the cell. For many students instruction about the cell may end with the textbook. But should it? How many high school biology textbooks are up-to-date on findings in genetic-biology? How many discuss cloning? Dare we let high school students graduate without finding out about these social and biological events which they later may need to consider when making adult decisions that could propel them into a grave new world of monsters or of controlled thought? Already scientists are sounding warnings about the need for legislation to regulate the applications of biological research. What are we teaching students now about the part they will inherit in making these decisions?

Here is another example: How many current science textbooks say something about an item as new as lunar science? For four years we have been able to read a great deal about it in newspapers, but we need to read more. With a space station imminent, with an international space probe planned for 1975, with Pioneer 10 speeding toward an unknown destination outside the solar system, can we truthfully say students are being exposed to what they need to know about their relation to this new world, if they don't have access to the print which allows them more time to consider the implications of space life—more time than is provided through sketchy TV and radio news programs? Late information is best provided through newspapers while the new textbooks are being written.

What about history and literature books which may ignore the offerings of minorities? Are students adequately prepared in human relations when they do not know that American Indians Chief Joseph and Sequoya were respectively an eloquent orator and a renowned linguist? That Phyllis Wheatley was a young, black slave-poet honored by both George Washington and George the Third? How many of our children, who are well acquainted with the ballad of Robin Hood through their English literature courses, have been exposed to his Spanish-American counterpart through the *corridos* of Gregorio Cortez? Most of these Americans are still unknown to students in schools in the United States and their contemporaries can be found in daily newspaper stories and features. Literature or "English" (not the most popular class in most schools) taught in relation to the newspaper arouses enthusiasm, not antagonism.

Another favorable aspect of the newspaper lies in the interesting reading it offers high school students. Many adolescents who will not read books or magazines will read newspapers. Thus, reading skills, which must be practiced if they are to be developed, can be taught from the print in newspapers just as well as from the print in workbooks and other more traditional materials. Some teachers say reading skills can be taught better through newspapers and cite, as evidence of their success, the presence of students in their classes. If use of the newspaper can cut down on absenteeism and use of books cannot, let us then try using the newspaper.

Comprehension skills are improved when a student reads regularly and extensively. Further, his comprehension of new materials depends largely upon what he already knows when he encounters the unfamiliar. Students who read very little, bring very little to the interpretation of symbols on the page being read. So to be a good reader, a student first must read. Teachers must give the student those materials he *will* read in order to stimulate continued reading.

One of the most outstanding benefits of the newspaper in the classroom, however, is the amount of free help—fringe benefits—given teachers by the newspaper publisher. To start with, most papers can be purchased in quantity by schools for half the newsstand price. In addition, the newspaper publisher offers frequent institutes and workshops which demonstrate how to use his product in the classroom. Many of these conferences offer graduate credit to teachers who take the courses under the sponsorship of local universities.

During the summer of 1972, the *Chicago Sun-Times* offered a two-day workshop in cooperation with the National College of Education in Chicago. The course was so popular that after applications from 150 teachers were accepted, more than 600 additional applications were turned down, due to lack of space and instructors. The *Chicago Tribune* offered a similar program in conjunction with Governor's State University at Park Forest, Illinois. Many metropolitan newspapers offer other similar courses in cooperation with local universities and colleges. In May 1972, the State Department of Public Instruction for Indiana, in conjunction with the Indiana Press Association, sponsored a two-day Institute for 50 of its Language Arts Supervisors at Indianapolis.

Along with formal instruction, newspaper publishers often print pamphlets and monographs on special reports prepared by staff writers, covering a wide range of topics centered around school projects such as hunger, poverty, mental health or concerning the Afro-American, the American Indian, the Chicano, and persons from India, China, and Latin America. These brochures offer up-to-date reporting, written in a readable style by professional writers, many of whom have won outstanding awards in the newspaper world.

Most newspapers also periodically reprint famous front pages for free distribution to schools. Some newspapers offer films and filmstrips for free use by schools which subscribe to their services.

A further indication of the attraction which newspapers hold for students and teachers lies in the fact that traditional textbook publishers often adopt the newspaper format for presentation of their product.

D. C. Heath, for example, with its Urban Reading Program, presents some of its materials in tabloid size and liberally illustrates them with photographs and text especially designed to resemble materials of the press. Charles E. Merrill has a series on American history which presents actual newspaper reprints of materials dating from 1841 (Westward Expansion) to 1939 (the Great Depression and the New Deal). They say, "For students, reading history from actual newspapers of the day transforms what has happened into what is happening." Along with this history of a past day, students have a chance to read the comics, the sports stories, and other features of that time. Similarly, the American Revolution with maps, engravings, and interviews is presented in tabloid form by Kubilius and Company.

Several years ago Portal Press adopted the newspaper format and technique in its Springboard program (later taken over by Noble and Noble). The *Rome Weekly,* for example, carries a story about the fire which killed thousands of people. It also includes interviews with prominent citizens about causes of the fire and reports on the Emperor who denies having anything to do with it but concedes that the fire probably will now permit him to construct a more beautiful city.

All of this adds up to the suggestion that use of the newspaper, generally ignored in most schools and even banned in some, is now due for a reevaluation.

We now are led to the question: If newspapers are so great, why have they been bypassed by schools for such a long time? One answer seems to lie in an attitude some people have acquired that newspapers aren't reliable, they are sensational, they are too cheap to contain good reading material, or they are somehow subversive.

Such outdated historical attitudes may reflect impressions of the early days of printing when the first newspapers were only broadsides or pamphlets which exaggerated descriptions of unusual events such as coronations, plagues, shipwrecks, fires, or hangings. These little papers often were hawked in the streets by persons who could not read but, nonetheless, knew how to attract the attention of eager listeners. As time passed, other subjects emerged as newsworthy. The most powerful attention-getter was politics; and thus the political pamphlet, later to become the idea of the free press, was born. The political pamphlet really came into its own during the seventeenth and eighteenth centuries when monarchies throughout the Western world were being challenged. At that time the pamphlet (or newspaper) was viewed as a very dangerous thing. The king was afraid of it because it wanted his throne—or his head. The people, though fascinated by its heretical ideas about equality and humanity, also were frightened, for the political pamphlet was almost as threatening to the life and security of the person who read it or listened to it being read, as it was to the person who wrote it. Unfounded as it may be, some of this tradition of fear and doubt still lurks in the attitudes people have today toward newspapers.

Another reason newspapers have been ignored by schools is that administrators and teachers continue to judge them by what they *were* rather than by what they *are* today. A glimpse of just how much newspapers have changed in one generation can be obtained by reviewing some of Dale's predictions (3) about the future of the newspaper when he wrote, in 1941, about what the needs would be in twenty-five years. Among other things, Dale predicted that the newspaper of the future would be: 1) More concerned with the needs of its customers, 2) involved with consumer education, 3) manned by better personnel, 4) easier to read, and 5) read by a populace with a higher than average education.

Time has proved Dale's predictions remarkably accurate. Newspapers are indeed more readable today. They have more pictures, they are more socially involved in their readers' lives, and they present *why* it happened as well as *how* it happened. If, after contrasting the paper of the seventies with the paper of the forties, a teacher still thinks newspapers never change, he should go to a library and spend an hour or two with some papers fifty, seventy-five, or one hundred years old. He will come away amazed at the changes which have been made. Today's newspaper has come a long way from its humble beginnings more than four centuries ago; but now, as then, it fulfills a need people have for knowing. As such, the newspaper should not be denied to anyone, regardless of age.

If we would like to introduce a current and inexpensive source of print into our schools and to our students, we can address ourselves to the newspaper as it exists today. Except for a piece of chalk, no other item for school use is so cheap and yet so adaptable. Once teachers start using the newspaper, they do not want to give it up.

And the students? Well, they are grouchy if by chance the paper is late or, horror of horrors, does not arrive at all because a substitute delivery man left it at the wrong school—their rival up the road five miles or so! Is today's student, who does not read, who will not read, who says he cannot read, telling us something?

references

1. American Newspaper Publishers Association, Box 17407, Dulles International Airport, Washington, D.C., 20041.
2. Cheyney, Arnold. *Teaching Reading Skills Through the Newspaper.* Newark, Delaware: International Reading Association, 1971, vi.
3. Dale, Edgar. "Newspapers Face the Future," *How to Read a Newspaper.* Glenview, Illinois: Scott, Foresman, 1941, 125.
4. *Education U.S.A.,* December 13, 1971, 3.
5. Johnson, Laura S. "The Newspaper: A New Textbook Every Day," *Journal of Reading,* November and December 1969.

Nonprint media can act as stimuli in motivating and developing a child's own language potential, thereby assisting the child in experiencing a relationship between the spoken and written word and life situations that are interesting and exciting.

use of nonprint media in language development

r. phillip carter
halifax, nova scotia

No one is likely to argue with the statement that language is at the heart of the education process. In fact, almost all the connotations of our terms *knowledge* and *education* are linguistic. It is the language process that enables us to run the eye of the mind over our perceptions, to codify experience, and, therefore, to learn. Whether we experience some aspect of the physical, biological, or social environment directly or indirectly, in either cognitive or affective ways, most often it is the vehicle of language—spoken, written, or gestured—which endows our experience with meaning. And we must keep in mind that *meaning* is essentially idiosyncratic in that it resides in a particular individual as a unique function of his experiences and the particular ways in which he has classified those experiences. So it is with the concepts which emerge as a result of this codifying process. For example, my concept of *stone* may not be precisely your concept of *stone* because my experience with stones may be vastly different than yours. The scar on my forehead is one experience, for instance. Meaning then is in people, not in words, phrases, or sentences. Ames' early studies in perception make this thought abundantly clear.

Without extensive thought, it should be obvious to us that children come to school with unique meanings as well as unique language patterns with which to describe those meanings. Into this anarchic linguistic universe we introduce a relatively standardized educational program—an enterprise which might perhaps be likened to a project for organizing the ocean. This abrasive juxtaposition of formal and spontaneous systems can, and often does, lead to what might be termed linguistic alienation.

the three r's—reality, relevance, and reading

There is ample evidence that many children do find themselves in a linguistically foreign environment in school. In other words, the language of the home and of their peers may differ significantly from the language of the basal reader and that of the teacher. This point is made quite poignantly when Wentworth tells Fader (4) "Sure I can read. I been able to read ever since I can remember. But I ain't never gonna let them know, on accoun' of iff'n I do I'm gonna have to read all that crap they got."

Upon hearing a supposedly illiterate boy read a passage from *Born Free,* Fader assumed the existence of a vast number of children who "cautiously enter the house called literacy—even if by the back door—and discover floors awry, mirrors crazed, and furniture built to serve other creatures. Recognizing a hostile environment, they retreat through doors and windows and have been retreating ever since." In his book, *Interpretation in Teaching* (15), Richards points to the trivial ways in which the schools go about studying language—ways which have no connection with life's experiences. He explains that the study of language is actually the study of our ways of living, the ways in which we interact with our environment, and the ways we perceive reality. Richards' statement is as relevant today as it was in 1938. The meaningful way to study and develop language facility in children, then, is in terms of the relationship of language to reality.

In telling of his sojourn to Garnet-Patterson Junior High, Fader relates many examples of language differences, but he also invites us —indeed, pleads with us—to recognize the vitality and validity of each child's language. Carney (2) describes the language teacher's role as, "not so much to inculcate 'good' English as to help the child to use [his own unique language] and express his experience in increasingly complex and sophisticated ways. . . . It is this sharing, and encouraging, of the child's growing language ability, that really counts." The value of using the real language of children resides in the fact that it is familiar, concrete, and spontaneous.

Using Nonprint Media

By way of illustrating the application of these views regarding language learning—that it must develop organically from each child's unique linguistic patterns and that it must be constantly related to reality—I shall describe two ways in which nonprint media were used to stimulate and develop sensory perception and provide rich and individually motivating activities and personally relevant language experiences.

how can nonprint media help?

One would have thought that, given the media-oriented world we live in, volumes would now have been written on the use of nonprint media in developmental reading programs. But apart from such treatments as those of Palmatier (12, 13), Artley (1), Karlin (10), and Spache (16)—mostly examinations of research of the machine versus non-machine variety—one searches the literature in vain for any comprehensive discussions and, although Hughes' book *Aids to Reading* (8) is quite complete, it would appear that the subject is still anyone's oyster.

Perhaps a distinction should be made here. I am not concerned with media which attempt to teach reading directly; these are discussed by Palmatier (13) and their use and effects in a developmental reading program should be well-known. Described in this paper are ways in which, as a medium, anyone of the nonprint media (audio- and videotapes, film, filmstrips, slides, records, or magic) can act as 1) a stimulus in motivating and developing a child's own language potential, 2) a catalyst for the imagination, and 3) a spur for creative thinking which would lead to further language inquiry and activity—the end result hopefully would be a greater interest in reading and a stronger desire to read. These examples indicate ways of assisting children and adolescents in experiencing a relationship between the spoken and written word and life situations that interest and excite them.

Goodman (6) writes, "If the child is reading material which deals with familiar situations and ideas, and this material is written in a language which is like his own oral language, then he can bring all of his language strength to bear on the task."

example 1: stones, cones, and bones

The ocean is one feature of the natural environment that is handy to most Nova Scotians, and the shore is a fascinating potpourri of "pick-me-ups." Just check the pockets of any child who has been there. For the five- and six-year-olds of St. Patrick's Elementary School, it is no less intriguing. With Kodak Instamatics, Ann Hughes set off with her class for the "kingdom by the sea." Sights they saw, smells they smelled, things they felt, sounds they heard, and even various tastes they experienced were all recorded on slides and audiotapes. The children made slides of what *they* saw and what *they* wanted to record. They were very observant and, being closer to the ground, often saw things that an adult might miss. The greatest excitement was not the experience of taking the slides but, back in the classroom, identifying the "ones you took" after they had been developed.

Aims of the Trip

1. To provide the children with firsthand experiences within their natural environment which could serve as touchstones for innumerable activities related to the entire curriculum.
2. To give the children an opportunity to express themselves freely in a familiar and related atmosphere—the seashore.
3. To give them a greater awareness of themselves through all their senses.
4. To give them a greater awareness of their environment and the world around them.
5. To bring their environment into the classroom in order to make the four walls less visible—literally, as you will see by the slides, and figuratively.
6. To give the children a greater appreciation of their own worth by involving them in all aspects of the trip. They answered the questions: Where shall we go? What shall we do? What shall we bring back? What shall we see, hear, smell, taste, and touch? And, what shall we tell?

The children's comments were recorded on tape as they described their experiences while on the trip; the tapes were transcribed later for use in the classroom. When the slides were developed and first shown in class, the children's comments were again recorded. Thereafter, each time any of the children wanted to relive that particular experience, they had as vivid and familiar reminders the slides, the audiotapes, and their language in printed form.

Stimulating, recording, and using the children's language were not the only purposes of the trip. Even more important were the resulting informal learning activities that grew out of the trip and which served to integrate the language arts with the entire curriculum. It can be seen from the following brief outline that the entire curriculum "went on the trip."

Class Work Before Going to Point Pleasant Park
- Study the table map of the city (made by the class) with important places of interest marked
- Trace route to be taken, marking the bus number and route on table map
- List places to be seen on the way to the park
- List things to be seen or collected at the park
- Discuss social behavior to be used away from school
- Introduce trip vocabulary in conversation—bus, fare, park, waves, beach, sand, rocks, grass, path, route, collections, driftwood, storms, ships, cargo

Class Work at Point Pleasant Park
- Observe
- Collect
- Experience and describe different earth textures such as sand, driftwood, bark, stones
- Share things of interest
- Listen to different sounds
- Learn about conservation
- Make decisions and choices
- Carefully observe and record the environment on tape and film

Class Work after Visiting Point Pleasant Park
1. Language Arts
- Discuss the journey, retracing the trip for sequence work
- Encourage children to originate stories about the trip
- Examine collections, compare textures of similar things, and discuss how to organize collections
- Answer questions such as: What is driftwood? How did it get on the beach? What is it like to be in a storm?
2. Numbers
- Weigh and measure the collections
- Find shapes
- Count
- Sort objects into sets—rough/smooth, big/little, colors
- Make line graphs showing largest collections
3. Science
- Collect living material
- Notice signs of spring
- Discuss movement of waves
- Leave salt water and fresh water on a saucer for evaporation

- Watch different materials dropped in a jar of water
- Observe things that float or sink

4. Social Studies
- Follow journey on the map
- List places seen on the way
- Discuss ships in the harbor and what they might have brought in or taken away

5. Art/Handwork
- Make a bus from boxes and use it in number work for giving change
- Paint pictures
- Use part of the collections in a mural
- Make sand pictures

6. Music/Drama
- Demonstrate sounds by rubbing different materials together
- Use water in bottles to make sounds
- Pretend to be waves in a storm and in calm
- Become sailors by pulling up anchors

Obviously, the number and types of activities that could follow such a trip are limited only by the imaginations of the teacher and students.

example 2: the medium of magic

No one had heard of Zoave, and it really didn't matter to the children or to the teacher. What did matter was the delightful excitement of the children as they reacted to forty minutes of homespun magic and the language that came forth. One five-year-old child related the following:

> I liked the magic and when the flower bent and you sat on your hat. We don't want you to sit on it any more because you might flatten it down and have to get glue and a hammer to fix it. I liked you. Thanks for the magic.
>
> Roger

We were particularly interested in recording the children's spontaneous explanations as to how a particular effect occurred. These recordings were then used as part of the language arts materials. One of the particularly fascinating aspects of this experience was noting the children's extensive use of logic as they tried to explain what had happened. Their inductive reasoning, creative imagination, and spontaneity would have inspired even the great Houdini.

The experience was also used for art expression, writing, and story discussions dealing with the supernatural. Again, the purpose was to capitalize on a child's natural interests and curiosity through the use of nonprint media (magic seems to qualify) and thereby provide a "real live" stepping stone for many integrated curriculum activities.

At the upper elementary and junior high level the film, "Ghost Stories of Nova Scotia," was added to the magic along with a great deal of printed material on the folklore and legends of Nova Scotia. The material for the film was gathered by our Lady of the Legends, Dr. Helen Creighton, and produced by CBC for television. Its use in the classroom promoted extensive reading, writing, story-gathering, and story-telling activities. The literature and language that the students gathered from their own environment were then incorporated into the language arts program, along with slides and tape recordings of tales told by persons of another generation. An invitation to produce radio broadcasts added a tremendous inducement to the students to create, organize, express, and relive familiar and vital language experiences. Remember, language has no meaning apart from the experiences of the user. Here again, with the aid of nonprint media, students were encouraged to use their developing language more effectively in communicating, thinking, and learning.

example 3: from rock to reading

The last example deals with developmental reading at the senior high level. At a regional vocational school, students had been grouped for reading and language instruction according to their scores on a highly verbal group intelligence test and a standardized reading test. Group one was the lowest; group three was supposedly the best; and group two was somewhere in between—a neat arrangement. With workbooks and programed materials, group one was out to slay the past pluperfect. Group two was busily avoiding dangling participles and hoisting commas around the ends of parenthetical clauses. Group three was innocently and blissfully using "the" language, even though it wasn't their own. Now apart from the program being upside down and inside out—that is, the students' "in" language was out—and having a Pygmalion in every classroom, nothing else much was wrong. (Someone should create a coat of arms for education with "the Hawthorne" rampant and "the learning" dormant and present it to schools which insist on doing things backwards.) Anyway, my invitation read, "We would like you to talk to the students on the value of reading." My first reaction was "okay, sure." My second was "hey, wow, you fool." And the closer it came to D-day (that's D for delivery) the more foolish I felt; however, the die was cast. The day before I was to change the course of their lives by imparting my wisdom regarding the nature of reading, I threw up or out what little I had prepared and began frantically collecting resources. The first item I grabbed was George Harrison's three-record album, "All Things Must Pass." I felt better already. And after we had played several favorite student selections—"Run of the Mill," "My Sweet Lord," "Isn't It a Pity?"—I felt even better, for I knew I was on the right track. We discussed the differences between rock-n-roll and folk rock and examined the social commentaries, anxieties, and frustrations embodied in the lyrics relative to such issues as the meaninglessness of school, pollution and destruction of the environment, never-ending war, love and sexuality, the hypocrisy of justice, the degradation of poverty, and many more—all topics seldom studied in school. But they they seldom show up in the anthologies either.

In each case our encounter with a topic began with nonprint media and progressed to print. We began the topic of "man's inhumanity to man" with a discussion of the movies, *A Patch of Blue, Soldier Blue,* and *Little Big Man;* went to recorded poems by Carl Sandburg and Langston Hughes; played records by George Harrison, Neil Diamond, and Bruce Cockburn and recordings by Martin Luther King and John F. Kennedy. After this, we looked at the writings of Eldridge Cleaver, Langston Hughes, LeRoi Jones, James Baldwin, Leonard Cohn, and June Jordan. After listening to and feeling the sounds of the language, the printed form—*Bury My Heart at Wounded Knee, Soul on Ice, Fire Down Below,* and *A Dream Deferred*—enjoyed a warmer reception.

The topic, "hypocrisy of justice," involved the movies, *To Kill a Mockingbird, The Anderson Tapes,* and *The New Centurion;* some records by Johnny Cash, Bob Dylan, and Joan Baez; the novels, *To Kill a Mockingbird, The Godfather,* and *The Boss;* and some of the poetry of Bob Dylan.

Some people may think this is an unnecessarily oblique approach to reading. In comparison with more than one venerable methodology for teaching reading, it is indeed so. But in teaching as in every other kind of seduction, the longest way around often turns out to be the shortest way home. The correct methodology is not the neatest methodology but the one that works. And in this little adventure, time passed unnoticed for the students in all three classes and for myself. Reading acquired value for these students when it became associated with other forms of communication which they themselves had chosen because of relevance to the realities of their own personal experiences. When students sensed the power of reading to satisfy their own personal needs, reading became no great chore.

I happen to believe that this indirect approach from actuality is the most vital approach to reading, but perhaps I am overly affected by poems such as the one written by an "incurable" boy in a remedial class:

> I can't read the books we use
> My brain goes blank
> My eyes won't fuse
> The teacher gives me every test
> Ah, go away and let me rest
> For what does she do
> When she gets the score
> She puts me out and shuts the door
> I never hear of it again
> Until it comes next grade and then
> The teacher finds that I can't read
> And so she proceeds with haste and speed
> To find another test for me
> Ah, go away and let me be.

references

1. Artley, A. Sterl. *Trends and Practices in Secondary School Reading.* Newark, Delaware: International Reading Association, 1968.
2. Carney, Janet C. "Children's Language is Real," *Nova Scotia Journal of Education,* 22 (Winter 1972-1973), 26.
3. Carroll, John B. "Words, Meanings, and Concepts," *Harvard Educational Review,* 34 (Spring 1964), 178-202.
4. Fader, Daniel. *The Naked Children.* New York: Macmillan, 1971.
5. Goodman, Kenneth S. "Reading: The Key Is in Children's Language," *Reading Teacher,* March 1972.
6. Goodman, Kenneth S. "The Language Children Bring to School: How to Build on It," *Grade Teacher,* 26 (March 1969), 135-142.
7. Goodman, Yetta, and Carol Burke. "Do They Read What They Speak?" *Grade Teacher,* 26 (March 1969), 144-150.
8. Hughes, John M. *Aids to Reading.* London: Evans Brothers, 1970.

9. Joos, Martin. "Language and the School Child," *Harvard Educational Review,* 34 (Spring 1964), 203-210.

10. Karlin, Robert. "Machines and Reading: A Review of Research," *Clearinghouse,* 32 (1958), 349-352.

11. Menosky, Dorothy, and Kenneth S. Goodman. "Unlocking the Program," *Instructor,* March 1971, 44-46.

12. Palmatier, Robert A. "Automation and Reading: A Perspective," *Journal of Reading Behavior,* 3 (Spring 1971).

13. Palmatier, Robert A. "The Role of Machines in the Reading Process," in Howard A. Klein (Ed.), *The Quest for Competency in Teaching Reading.* Newark, Delaware: International Reading Association, 1972, 269-279.

14. Postman, Neil, and Charles Weingartner. *Teaching as a Subversive Activity.* New York: Delacorte Press, 1969.

15. Richards, I. A. *Interpretation in Teaching.* New York: Harcourt, Brace, 1938.

16. Spache, George D. "A Rationale for Mechanical Methods of Improving Reading," in O. S. Causey (Ed.), *Significant Elements in College and Adult Reading Improvement,* Seventh Yearbook of the National Reading Conference for College and Adults. Fort Worth, Texas: Texas Christian University, 1958, 115-132.

In utilizing teacher-made materials, Charry points out the necessity of controlling readability. Recommendations are stated to enable the classroom teacher to modify the readability of material without distorting the content.

controlling readability factors of teacher-made materials

lawrence b. charry
philadelphia, pennsylvania

There is an ever present need for controlling the readability of materials that the teacher creates in the day-to-day routine of the classroom. These written communications between teacher and students must be understood immediately, even in a classroom comprised of students with widely varying reading capabilities.

The limitations of all the students must be kept in mind as materials are being prepared. While the remedial readers have very specific needs that must be met, those readers at the corrective and developmental level also must be considered. Not all students have the same grasp of concepts, and students have varied levels of ability in the different content areas.

controls needed at all levels

A tremendous amount and variety of reading material exists at the beginning reading level. Accompanying the basic material is a large body of easy-to-read supplementary materials.

This does not, however, preclude the necessity for and desirability of classroom-generated materials. The readability of these materials should be controlled by the teacher. For example, when a student dictates material for an experience chart, the teacher should try to record as many words as are within the child's reading capability, as opposed to the much larger number of words that are part of the child's spoken vocabulary.

As students progress to the intermediate levels and beyond, the demand for controlled basic and supplementary materials increases as the supply of available materials diminishes. The students are more deeply involved in the content areas of science and social studies, and many difficult and abstract concepts are encountered for the first time. Students at all levels should be provided with materials which present no reading roadblocks. To learn with the maximum amount of efficiency, the student must be free to concentrate on learning new ideas without becoming mired in reading comprehension problems.

Specifically, a seventh grade student who reads at the fifth grade level should be given teacher-made science materials that are one grade lower in terms of readability. Of course, the new concepts would be among those included in the seventh grade curriculum. It becomes necessary, however, to be judicious in terms of selecting the most important of these concepts. The amount of explanatory text that is used should be sufficient to assure that these concepts are understood satisfactorily.

variables in readability

In the writing of carefully controlled materials, two of the variables most often considered are the length and complexity of the sentences and the vocabulary load.

The careful control of sentence length is essential at the beginning reading level. Teachers often ask what sentence lengths are to be used. Arbitrary criteria should not be set up, but some rule of thumb figures often can be of considerable help.

A reasonable suggestion would be to have an average of six to ten words per sentence at the elementary level; nine to twelve words per sentence at the intermediate grade level; and ten to fifteen words per sentence at junior high level. Some latitude should be allowed at the high school level, although there probably should be a maximum of fifteen words per sentence.

More important than the actual number of words per sentence is the necessity for varying the sentence length. If the student is given a long sentence to digest, a short explanatory sentence can follow. This will help to explain the previous statement and also give the student a breathing space.

Readability of Teacher-Made Materials

The control of the complexity of the sentence is also more important than the sentence length. Sentences should not have too many qualifying clauses and phrases or too many interruptions with parentheses and dashes. When a large number of words—such as interrupting phrases and clauses—separates the subject from the predicate, the content may be hard to follow. While the sentence structure should be varied, this should not be done at the expense of the student's ultimate understanding of the text.

Another important variable to be considered is the vocabulary load. Most of the widely used readability formulas are based on a word list, and the grade score of a sample is dependent upon the number of words *not* included in the basic word list.

The words that are not on the basic lists are termed *hard* or *unfamiliar.* When they are concepts that are difficult to understand, they must be clarified. This should be done in simple terms so that the explanation does not become more difficult than the concept.

In biology, a statement may indicate that cells *divide by mitosis.* The meaning should immediately be spelled out that one cell becomes two identical cells. Thus, the definition is provided directly following the introduction of the concept to be learned.

Sometimes individual words which are fairly simple in meaning become difficult concepts when combined. *Gross national product* is such an example. It is to be noted that this is a critical concept and therefore it must be explained as fully as possible.

Words which are changed from one part of speech to another can also cause difficulty. *Traditional teaching* and *feathered friends* are examples of situations wherein the nouns, *tradition* and *feather,* become adjectives; such changed words may be hard to understand.

Special attention should be given to words that are not used in their most familiar context. When a child is told, "store things in your memory," the word *store* becomes difficult to comprehend.

In the sentence, "Hills and turns make the going rough," the word *going* becomes somewhat obscure. Care should be taken with words that shift in meaning. *Going* is most familiar as a verb. Changing the part of speech can cause confusion. These examples show only a few of the situations in which intrinsically simple words can become difficult to understand when they are combined and changed.

In addition to sentence lengths and vocabulary lists, readability formulas involve other factors. The Lorge formula (7) includes an additional variable, prepositional phrases. Some educators assume that prepositional phrases indicate greater complexity of sentences. This may not always be true, since some phrases are extremely easy (*to the store, on the table*), and others may be very difficult (*in truth, under duress*). However, the Lorge formula is useful because it bridges the gap between the upper level of the Spache formula and the lower level of the Dale-Chall formula. Neither of these formulas is quite satisfactory at the fourth grade level.

The Flesch (*4*) and the Fry (*5*) formulas take into consideration sentence length and polysyllabic words. While, in the long run, polysyllabic words are generally more difficult than one-syllable words, there are pitfalls to the use of these formulas. A syllable count does not tell the teacher which specific words are difficult. No accounting is given of words not on the basic list, a basic necessity in controlling the readability of materials.

simplifying readability computations

Many teachers become bogged down in the computations of readability formulas, even though ready made tables simplify the final steps. The following suggestions may be of assistance in providing a better understanding of the influence of the variables on the total grade score.

Generally, the Spache (*8*) and the Dale-Chall (*3*) are the most popular and widely used formulas throughout the grades. The Spache formula encompasses the first to low fourth grades, and the Dale-Chall goes from third to twelfth grades. According to the Spache formula, to get a picture of the effect of sentence length on readability, a sample will have a grade placement of 3.0 if it has an average sentence length of 11 words and 7 hard words (out of 100). If the average sentence length increases by one word to 12, with the same 7 hard words, the grade placement then becomes 3.1.

Using the Dale-Chall formula, a sample of 100 words will have a grade score of 5.0, when the average sentence length is 12, and the number of unfamiliar words is 5. If the average sentence length is increased by one word to 13, and the number of difficult words remains the same, the grade level then becomes 5.1.

With both the Spache and the Dale-Chall formulas, it can be seen that each word added to the sentence length contributes one-tenth of a grade to the readability level. (These figures are approximations; final scores may show a slight increase because of rounding off.)

To get the picture of the effect of vocabulary on readability, the following illustrations should be helpful: With the same sample of the Spache formula indicated above (sentence length of 11 with 7 hard words), an additional hard word raises the grade placement from 3.0 to 3.1. It can be seen that each additional hard word contributes one-tenth of a grade to the readability level.

With the sample of the Dale-Chall formula presented previously (sentence length of 12 with 5 unfamiliar words), 3 additional unfamiliar words increase the grade level to 6.0. On the average, the readability level is increased about one grade with the addition of 3 unfamiliar words. (Again, this is an approximation, since the rounding off procedure sometimes affects the score slightly.)

use of word lists

Many of the readability formulas provide basic word lists that are of assistance to the teacher who writes original materials; however, the word lists now in use need revision.

The Dale-Chall list of 3,000 words dates back to the 1940s. The 769 Dale word list, also published in the 1940s, is used in the Lorge formula. An updated version of the Dale 769 word list, by Clarence Stone, was published in 1956 and is used in the Spache formula.

Two word frequency lists which have appeared recently should be of tremendous help in modernizing word lists. Kucera and Francis (6) developed a very comprehensive frequency list in 1967.

In 1971 the *American Heritage Word Frequency Book* (2), was developed by Carroll, Davies, and Richman. This book gives frequency counts by grade, starting from grade three, as well as by total number of occurrences. Although the book costs $25, every school should purchase at least one copy because of its unquestionable value.

Any discussion of readability must take into account the need to write questions clearly. Poor readers are already handicapped by their inability to grasp written material. Therefore, they should not be given the additional burden of responding to test questions which they cannot read. Students who misunderstand the questions cannot possibly answer them correctly. Tests should be designed to minimize reading difficulty, so that a student's reading problems do not interfere with the accurate measurement of his subject-matter knowledge.

assisting the classroom teacher

The reading teacher should always be available to assist the classroom teacher in the preparation of material. In this role, after examining a first draft of the materials, the reading teacher makes written or oral recommendations on readability. The classroom teacher is then able to prepare a more polished version, incorporating changes that are based on the reading teacher's comments.

These comments should never be in the nature of alterations to the intrinsic content of the material. (In many cases, particularly at the high school level, the content will be outside the reading teacher's expertise.) Instead, comments should point out stumbling blocks that students might encounter because the material is too difficult to read.

Relying on the reading teacher's recommendations, and on her own specialized knowledge, the classroom teacher can modify the readability of material without distorting its content. After the content teacher has been alerted to possible sources of reading difficulty in her writing, she can develop materials better adapted to the reading capabilities of her students.

Once the prepared materials are satisfactory, the cloze technique (1) may be applied. This technique is used for materials that the student has never read and may provide a further indication of appropriateness of the material. In the cloze technique, every fifth word is omitted and the student must supply the correct word for this space. If the material is on a student's reading level, he should have no trouble supplying the missing words. The teacher is assured that the material is on target when a satisfactory number of written-in answers are found to be correct.

The search for appropriately controlled materials is endless. The range of published materials will never be broad enough to encompass all students' needs. Often, the only answer will be to develop teacher-generated materials.

Formulas and techniques are only guides. The teacher must determine how well students work in the actual classroom situation and must make creative use of the formulas and techniques so that each student's needs are met.

Through the understanding of the variables in readability, and through continued efforts to control these variables more effectively, teachers can produce classroom materials which are interesting, informative, and highly readable.

references

1. Bormuth, John. "The Cloze Readability Procedure," *Elementary English,* 45 (April 1968), 429-436.

2. Carroll, John B., Peter Davies, and Barry Richman. *American Heritage Word Frequency Book.* New York: Houghton Mifflin and American Heritage, 1971.

3. Dale, Edgar, and Jeanne Chall. "A Formula for Predicting Readability," *Educational Research Bulletin,* 27 (January 21 and February 17, 1948), 11-20, 37-54.

4. Flesch, R. F. "A New Readability Yardstick," *Journal of Applied Psychology,* 32 (1948), 221-233.

5. Fry, Edward B. "A Readability Formula that Saves Time," *Journal of Reading,* 11 (1968), 513-516.

6. Kucera, Henry, and W. Nelson Francis. *Computational Analysis of Present Day American English.* Providence, Rhode Island: Brown University Press, 1967.

7. Lorge, Irving. *The Lorge Formula for Estimating Difficulty of Reading Materials.* New York: Teachers College Press, 1959.

8. Spache, George. *Good Reading for Poor Readers.* Champaign, Illinois: Garrard, 1970.

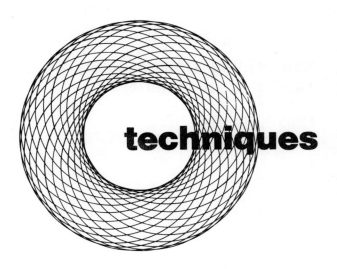

techniques

An *informal reading algorithm* is explained for the purpose of helping teachers above grade five determine the needs of pupils relative to a specific course, text, or subject.

determining student ability to read subject material

perry l. franklin
simon fraser university

Secondary teachers frequently ask, "What can I do with the students in my classes who can't read the assignments?" and "Can you suggest a list or program of materials that the low-achievers can use while the rest of the class does the assigned reading?"

the problem

The preceding typical statements ask the basic questions: How can I determine whether my students can handle the course content? If they cannot do the required work successfully, why can't they, and how can I remedy the problem?

Applying the Informal Reading Algorithm helps in 1) separating the students who can cope with normal text and other reading assignments from those who cannot, 2) placing students in one of the four categories shown at the second level of the algorithm, 3) assessing the entire class as a group, and 4) scoring and interpreting the results quickly.

phase I—group testing

The first major step is to administer the group tests suggested by the boxes at the first level of the algorithm. Beginning with *Evaluate*

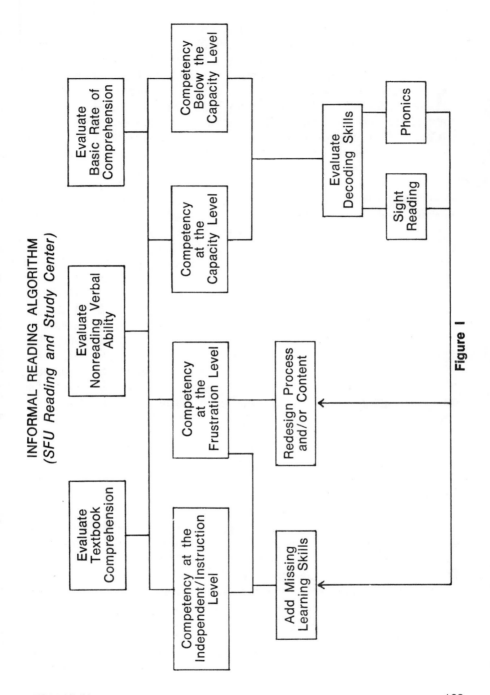

INFORMAL READING ALGORITHM
(SFU Reading and Study Center)

Figure I

Basic Rate of Comprehension, it is suggested that the Van Wagenen Rate of Comprehension Scale, Form D (*10*) be used. The writer agrees with Davis (*2*) that directions given to the student taking this test should make it clear that the time limit is short and that individual scores depend mainly on speed. This addition should be made by the test administrator. The Van Wagenen (VW) gives a standardized estimate of reading rate wherein the decoding and comprehension load are at grade four level. Also, it gives an indication of the mental age and grade level of the student. Working time is four minutes for this test.

The second group assessment area to be discussed is *Evaluate Nonreading Verbal Ability.* This instrument gives an indication of the student's level of vocabulary in relation to a standardized group when the decoding aspect of reading is clearly removed.

Basic Rate vs Aural Vocabulary. The test suggested for the evaluation of nonreading verbal ability is the Peabody Picture Vocabulary Test (*3*). This test is relatively easy to administer and score. Two useful areas that can be obtained from the PPVT are mental age and percentile rank of the student. Also the PPVT is recommended because it covers a wide range of mental ages from 1.9 years to 18.0 years.

Results of the VW and the PPVT can be used to determine the student's basic reading level in relation to his aural vocabulary level and the relation of these tests to his peers' abilities and expected grade level abilities. For example, the teacher can compare a student's ability to comprehend reading material at grade four level (VW) with his ability to comprehend orally presented material (PPVT).

The Informal Reading Inventory. The remaining step at level one of the algorithm is to decide how well the student is able to do the regularly prescribed course of study.

Here the writer suggests a group-administered Informal Reading Inventory (IRI) as suggested by Karlin (*6*) or Strang (*9*). A typical passage of about 250 words is chosen from the course text; then ten comprehension questions are written from it. It is at this point the teacher should consider his teaching (learning) objectives. Clarity in writing the questions also can be enhanced by referring to *Bloom's Taxonomy of Educational Objectives* (*1*). For example, if the teacher wants to teach more than straight recall (knowledge), he should write questions appropriate to other comprehension skills using Bloom's Taxonomy as a guide when he constructs the IRI.

Administering the Informal Reading Inventory. The students are given the text and a separate set of questions and told the purpose of the IRI. They are told that they will be timed on the straight reading of the selection, they will be responsible for answering questions after they have read the selection, and this will be timed. Students should be told that they may refer to the material while answering the questions but, of course, this must be a part of the total time it takes them to complete the IRI.

To facilitate timing, the students should begin together to read the text of the IRI. They should be instructed to turn the question sheet face up when they have finished reading the text and note on their paper the elapsed time, supplied by the teacher or by a timer. (Most students could time themselves if a large clock with a sweep second hand were available.) When they have finished answering the questions students should again write the total elapsed time on their papers. For example, if three minutes elapse as the student does the reading part of the IRI and if twenty minutes elapse as he completes the IRI questions, he would write *three* opposite Reading Time and *twenty* opposite Total Time. Clearly, the difference between the Reading Time and the Total Time is the time it took the student to work on the answer section.

phase II—placement

The second major step is to place the students in one of the four categories at the second level of the algorithm. First, the score on the comprehension part of the IRI should be interpreted by using the Reading and Listening levels as suggested by Zintz (*11*). The comprehension scores and reading rates should identify students at Independent and Instructional levels. Confirmation of this decision and verification of placement of the remaining students in the appropriate categories can be made by comparing 1) the reading rate on the Van Wagenen with the reading rate on the Informal Reading Inventory, 2) the mental age on the Peabody Picture Vocabulary Test with the mental age on the Van Wagenen, and 3) the percentile rank on the Peabody Picture Vocabulary Test with the student's comprehension on the Informal Reading Inventory. For example, if a student's reading rate on the IRI and the VW is in the lower half of the class and his comprehension on the IRI is around 50 percent, but his score on the PPVT is average, he could be placed at the Frustration Level. As a result of this placement, the teacher will realize that attention must be given to the length and content of the student's assignments. Another example is a problem student who scores lower than 50 percent on the IRI, low on the VW, but normal range on the PPVT; he is a candidate for the "Competency at the Capacity Level" box. That is, he is able to cope with the content of the curriculum if reading is not the major source of information. If the same student's results are also significantly low on the PPVT, his ability should be considered as being below the Capacity Level since there is a good chance he will not be able to cope with the normal curriculum at the normal rate regardless of the type of help given.

Decoding Skills. The students who appear to be at Capacity or Below Capacity levels as shown on the algorithm should have their decoding and basic reading skills tested individually. The writer suggests using the Roswell-Chall Diagnostic Reading Test, Form I to evaluate phonic abilities (8) and the Standardized Oral Reading Paragraphs (5) to estimate sight reading grade level. If the teacher prefers comprehension questions in conjunction with the oral reading, the Gray Oral Reading Tests (4) may be used.

A final note about use of the algorithm concerns the box labeled "Add Missing Learning Skills." All students will benefit from information about systematic methods of concentrating and remembering. As a process that will help the student learn the content, the writer suggests incorporating into the curriculum the study skills from one of the many good books dealing with the topic. An excellent example of such information is *Effective Study* by Robinson (7).

phase III—congruency

At this point the teacher should have the necessary information to think both inductively and deductively about the learning needs of the student; that is to say, what appears to be the need of the student, the teacher, and/or the curriculum and how much realignment is necessary in the three areas to best meet these needs.

conclusion

The writer has shown a method by which the classroom teacher at the postintermediate grade level can diagnose and begin prescribing for the reading and learning needs of a class. The method has as its goals the gathering of a maximum amount of decision-making information coupled with maximum ease of evaluation. It should be clear that such a pragmatic attempt must compromise both areas to some degree. The important thing is that the Informal Reading Algorithm does provide a workable model that can be upgraded or modified as the "fit" changes among the teacher, the student, and the curriculum.

references

1. Bloom, B. S. (Ed.). *Taxonomy of Educational Objectives: Handbook I, Cognitive Domain.* New York: McKay, 1956.
2. Davis, F. B. "Diagnostic Examination of Silent Reading Abilities," in O. K. Buros (Ed.), *Reading Tests and Review.* Highland Park: Gryphon Press, 1968.
3. Dunn, L. M. *Peabody Picture Vocabulary Test.* Circle Pines, Minnesota: American Guidance Service, 1965.
4. Gray, W. S. *Gray Oral Reading Tests.* Indianapolis: Bobbs-Merrill, 1963.
5. Gray, W. S. *Standardized Oral Reading Paragraphs.* Indianapolis: Bobbs-Merrill, 1959.
6. Karlin, R. *Teaching Elementary Reading: Principles and Strategies.* New York: Harcourt Brace Jovanovich, 1971, 53-59.
7. Robinson, F. P. *Effective Study* (rev. ed.). New York: Harper & Row, 1961.
8. Roswell, F. G., and J. S. Chall. *Roswell-Chall Diagnostic Reading of Word Analysis Skills.* New York: Essay Press, 1959.
9. Strang, R. "Informal Reading Tests in Each Subject," in L. M. Schell and P. C. Burns (Eds.), *Remedial Reading: Classroom and Clinic* (2nd ed.). Boston: Allyn and Bacon, 1972.
10. Van Wagenen, M. J. *Van Wagenen Rate of Comprehension Scale, Form D.* Minneapolis: Educational Test Bureau, 1953.
11. Zintz, M. V. *The Reading Process: The Teacher and the Learner.* Dubuque, Iowa: Wm. C. Brown, 1970, 52-55.

Karlin elaborates upon his belief that direct instruction in the reading of content materials in subject matter areas is better than an external and artificial effort to "teach comprehension skills" at the high school level.

developing comprehension skills in the high school student

robert karlin
queens college
city university of new york

At the outset, each of us should be clear about the messages conveyed by the topic of this presentation. Teachers do not improve the comprehension of their students. Instead, they help students develop abilities that could enable them to read with better understanding the information and ideas conveyed by authors of subject-oriented materials in literature, science, social studies, mathematics, health, home economics—in short, the books and reference sources, the newspapers and magazines they will be reading in and out of school. Moreover, weaknesses in comprehension which may be overcome through instruction have their origins in different sources. Therefore, diagnostic teaching requires that these be identified so that efforts to modify student behaviors will have a fair chance to succeed. Teachers will not conduct a lesson in reading comprehension; instead, they will concentrate on learning to establish purposes for reading, developing word competency, searching for surface and deeper meanings, and evaluating information and ideas gained through reading. To these we might add learning to locate, master, and retain information. Thus, we can establish discrete but related goals based upon established requirements and offer lessons to help students achieve them.

At this point it might be useful to differentiate between teacher guidance which is intended to help students read with greater comprehension those materials which serve current requirements and instruction that has as its long-term goal the development of skills and attitudes that will serve students' recurring needs—for example, when a teacher introduces difficult and unfamiliar vocabulary in advance of close reading, this meets the former purpose. When a teacher requires that students justify conclusions purportedly based on stated information, he could be developing long-term behaviors. Naturally, many strategies that help students overcome obstacles to comprehension might fulfill both objectives.

establishing reading purposes

Reading with a purpose is more efficient than reading without one. Students who read for specified reasons will be thinking as they are reading and not merely receiving information they are supposed to consume. The active reader has a problem he wishes to solve, but the passive reader is merely a receptacle for facts.

Many high school students report that they have trouble concentrating as they read assignments. They think about other matters, and as a result they understand less and remember little. Students who have a purpose for reading are bound to accomplish more than others who fail to identify one. Purposes serve to stimulate thoughtful reading. Teachers can promote this kind of reading by providing suitable motives for students to discuss and weigh. Readers who are exposed to such stimulation are more likely to ask themselves "What shall I look for?" or "How shall I read this material?" before beginning to read on their own than if they study in a setting which merely requires coverage of "the next ten pages" to be followed by discussion or a quiz.

Purposes for reading in subject areas do not always have to be teacher inspired if students are involved in solving problems that are thought provoking and challenging. The very nature of the problems-approach to learning encourages students to formulate questions. Thus, if a group in a history course is evaluating the effects of our foreign policy *vis-a-vis* the "third world" nations, they could establish the boundaries or framework that would elicit relevant information: What is our foreign policy toward the third world? How has this policy affected the politics and economics of these countries? Is this policy consistent with our declared positions on international cooperation and assistance? These and related questions serve as the purposes for which students will read in order to gather sufficient information for resolving basic problems.

The preview technique, which is part of the well-established SQ3R plan of study, is another means by which students can develop their own purposes for reading. By reading the chapter introduction or introductory paragraphs and reflecting upon the information to be covered, they can begin to relate what they know to the content that they will be reading. Thinking about the subject serves as a stimulant to productive reading; it also can help students to identify areas on which they might concentrate. Chapter subheads and illustrative materials provide additional insights into the nature and treatment of the content; both may suggest purposes for which reading will be undertaken. Students can be taught how to convert subheads into one or more questions. In biology, for example, *Controlling Harmful Plants* might be the subhead. This subhead might elicit purposes for reading in the form of questions such as: What types of plants are harmful? Why are these plants judged harmful? What measures can be taken to control them? Summaries usually contain general statements which the text clarifies. These, too, can become springboards for careful study. This survey—the examination of introductions, organizational features, and summaries—will enable students to obtain an overview of the problem; it also will provide a set for study.

developing vocabulary

Aside from technical words, there is a general vocabulary identified with all content subjects. Teachers are familiar with the problems that occur when word meanings are only vaguely understood and ideas are generated that have little relationship to the context. Studies show that all other conditions being equal, knowledge of word meaning seems to be the most important single factor that accounts for variability in reading comprehension.

It is not realistic to assume that we can teach students all the words they will need in order to read with understanding. A much better strategy is to teach them how to use their own and other resources in treating unfamiliar vocabulary. These resources include awareness of contextual and morphemic clues, multiple word meanings, figurative language, and dictionary usage.

To effect the greatest utilization of contextual aids, typical passages (experience, mood, definition, explanation, comparison, contrast) can be analyzed to discover relationships between the context clues they contain and the meanings of familiar and unfamiliar words.

Comprehension Skills at the High School Level

Once these relationships are established, students can apply this knowledge to new words in other settings. It is important, however, for students to realize that context clues do not always provide solutions to word meaning problems and that they will have to look elsewhere for solutions.

Morphemic clues, with or without context clues, may be sources of help. These are the clues contained in words themselves—roots, prefixes, suffixes, and compound word parts. Students can learn how to use the meanings that these convey by studying them through known words in context and later dealing with these morphemes in new words. This procedure is superior to one which offers long lists of word parts whose meanings students are expected to memorize and apply.

Helping students to distinguish between literal and figurative meanings of words is not difficult if throughout their reading activities, students have been encouraged to search for deeper meanings. Students will have heard and used figurative language, and these familiar expressions may be used to develop awareness of and reactions to words treated in special ways. Most efforts of this nature are reserved for times when students are reading materials that contain such words.

The study of multiple word meanings and the dictionary may be combined. If context and morphemic clues are lacking, students have to rely on using the dictionary to sort out the meanings of words that may be understood in one context but not in another. A simple way to help students ascertain appropriate meaning is to have them substitute different dictionary meanings for the unknown words and then decide through discussion which meanings best fit the context. It might be necessary on occasion to reword the dictionary meaning so that the substitution does not produce an awkward statement.

recognizing relationships (literal)

One measure of comprehension is the extent to which the reader sees relationships among ideas or how ideas go together. The ability to understand is increased by perception of the structure which ties a group of sentences together or by the recognition that no firm structure exists. Students who look for and recognize patterns of organization will begin to think about ideas as the author did. The closer the reader follows the author's thoughts, the greater will be his comprehension of them.

Paragraphs are organized in different ways. One type of organization serves to unify ideas that are closely related by expressing them in a distinct structure or format. The ways in which these ideas are expressed to convey their association are time order, enumeration, cause-effect, and comparison-contrast. A fifth structure, topical, may be discerned within each of the others. A second type of organization is used by authors to express functions. It is exemplified by paragraphs that *introduce* a reader to a subject, *illustrate* ideas that have been expressed in order to clarify them, *bridge* gaps between ideas, and *summarize* important points.

We can help students perceive the structure that writers use to give form to their ideas. A suitable way to do this is to cause them to think about the contents in specified ways by having them respond to questions which emphasize relationships. Thus, if students are tracing the developments that led to the discovery of photosynthesis, we could stress time-order relationships through such questions as: Approximately how long did it take scientists to discover and understand the process? Upon whose earlier studies did _____ base his experiments? If we ask students to read in order to find out what a given scientist discovered about the process, we are not directing attention to the structure in the way the other questions do. To stress cause and effect relationships, notice how the first set of questions serves this purpose, while the second set, though it covers similar content, fails to do so.

Why do we suggest that you are what you eat?
Why do nutritionists urge youth to "go easy" on candy,
  potato chips, and pop?
What food elements do our bodies require?
Which types of foods should you avoid?

For each organizational pattern, you can formulate questions that not only highlight information you believe students should master but also require them to think about the ideas, not in isolation, but in relationship to others. The immediate effect of this kind of reading guidance is improved comprehension. More important is the development of skills and attitudes which facilitate comprehension of materials read independently.

Functional paragraphs can be treated similarly. For example, you can direct students' attention to illustrative and summary types by raising questions about the content that require them to relate ideas and examples and find statements which convey the same or similar ideas. Questions that focus attention on related but different ideas through recognition of signposts—such as *however* and *on the other hand*—reveal the transitional nature of the material.

A related problem is the confusing syntactical structures that some sentences contain. Although single sentences are less likely to be misunderstood, some students may require help in analyzing and comprehending them. Students can be taught to identify the parts that contain the basic meanings: one which identifies the subject(s) and the other which provides information about the subject(s). All the other parts of the sentence contribute to the message conveyed, but they do not carry the basic information. Either by omitting these parts or by shifting them temporarily, we can underscore the fundamental parts:

Omit parts: The strands of the fungus [that grow over the surface of the leaf] then produce millions of spores [which appear as a powdery substance on the leaves].

Shift parts: At certain times of the year because of unsettled climatic conditions space explorations must be curtailed.

Once the basic information is recognized, the sentences may be reread in their original form for complete meaning.

Another way to attack a complex sentence is to analyze it for the different ideas it conveys. Several simple statements are contained in the following sentence:

A fragment of jawbone that appears to date early man back five and one-half million years has been discovered recently in the bush of Kenya by a group of Harvard scholars.

1. A fragment of jawbone has been discovered.
2. It has been discovered recently.
3. The fragment appears to date early man.

The sentence contains several separate ideas that students might not recognize. This form of analysis requires the reader to pay careful attention to each group of words that carries meaning and to the relationships that exist among the words. A rereading of the original sentence should then be more meaningful.

Still another source of confusion might be pronouns whose referents might be masked:

Trophy hunting by white men is no more popular with the Eskimos than the wasteful slaughter of the buffalo was with the American Indians. *It* seems to them a wasteful killing of an animal that they consider a resource.

Students can be taught to identify the word or words the pronoun represents by asking, in this instance, *what* seems to them a wasteful killing and substitute another word for the pronoun. This substitution will reveal whether the pronoun and referent are properly matched and if they are not, the restructured sentence will not make much sense within the framework of other sentences. Pronouns that represent ideas may be treated similarly.

recognizing relationships (inferential)

At the secondary level the ability to know what the writer means is no less important than to understand what he says. As with literal reading, teachers should know in behavioristic terms what inferential reading encompasses so that they will be goal oriented. To read inferentially is to draw conclusions, to make generalizations, to sense relationships, to predict outcomes, to realize an author's purpose. These are related reading tasks, for each one requires students to use whatever ideas and information they have in order to sense what the author means. The real objective of teaching students to read for deeper meanings is to instil the attitude that reading requires more than receiving surface messages and that reading involves thinking about other ideas the messages may convey.

A way to teach students to make inferences is to require them to respond in specified ways. Teachers may do this through questions and discussions that focus the readers' attention upon the ways in which they must think in order to move beyond the surface messages. Suitable questions can stimulate thinking because they require us to use what we already know—the surface messages—to read between the lines. If responses are discussed, analysis can reveal weaknesses in them and suggest more appropriate ways to deal with subsequent reading tasks.

If we are teaching students to draw some conclusions from a given passage, we may offer several possibilities and then have the students seek support for each from the information provided. The ensuing discussion would reveal why some conclusions are more valid than others, that more than one conclusion might be drawn, that some conclusions should be rejected because they lack support. We can direct students' attention to a series of statements in a passage and from these consider whether they permit us to draw specified conclusions or make firm generalizations from them. Similar treatments can be followed in assessing an author's purpose and attitudes. Questions such as "What parts of the passage suggest that the author believes . . . ?'' or ''What might you infer from these statements about the author?'' demonstrate to students the kinds of questions they must ask as they read on their own and how they must react to them.

Another aspect of drawing inferences is anticipating what kinds of information the author is likely to cover. Students may be taught to recognize signals that suggest what is ahead and to raise questions or make comments which can serve as additional purposes as they read. For example, when students read that the present administration *followed the basic foreign policy* developed by previous administrations, they can ask themselves, ''What policy?'' This anticipation serves as a stimulus for reviewing in their own minds what they already know and for readying themselves for possible answers to the question they asked. Students who learn to read this way will not suffer from lack of direction; instead, they will be alert to nuances which can promote comprehension.

evaluating ideas

To read critically is to understand more. Although critical evaluation occurs after the reader has grasped the author's ideas or gained information, it is a natural extension of reading for meaning. Many students have the ability to evaluate what they read but fail to do so. Of course, some lack background against which to weigh ideas or do not learn as quickly as others. But each can be encouraged to react to the extent that he can. Stated as behavioral objectives, students will learn to judge accuracy, distinguish between fact and opinion, recognize qualification, and perceive persuasion.

In order to reach these goals, students will engage in reading which requires a wide sampling of materials so that they can compare coverage for similarities and differences. They will study information obtained from several sources—such as text and reference sources, newspapers and magazines—with the intent of selecting relevant parts and of rejecting others. They will analyze the content of editorials and relate it to the presentation of news that purports to be factual. As students read in literature they will compare fictional characters with people they know, observe how similar themes are treated by different writers, and examine literary styles as means for achieving authors' purposes. In reading social studies, students will weigh the actions of government and its citizens, make or withhold recommendations on the basis of known information, recognize that some evidence is difficult to verify or to prove. In studying science they will identify what is known and what is unknown about the universe, evaluate the validity of changing concepts, judge explanations and proposals on scientific and moral grounds. In the other subject areas, they will examine with an equally critical attitude the content they learn.

Above all, we want to encourage a healthy skepticism and at the same time avoid intemperate behaviors. We can promote thoughtful evaluation by demonstrating the need for reading with an inquiring attitude and stressing the desirability of reaching judgments that are based upon valid information.

Practical suggestions for improving comprehension skills of intermediate level students are presented by Smith.

practical ideas for developing comprehension in content areas

zelda smith
northern kentucky state college

In Lewis G. Carroll's *Alice's Adventures in Wonderland,* Humpty Dumpty and Alice were involved in the following conversation: "When I use a word," Humpty Dumpty said in a rather scornful tone, "it means just what I choose it to mean—nothing more or less." "The question is," said Alice, "whether you can make words mean so many different things." "The question," said Humpty Dumpty, "is which is to be master—that's all."

Our question here is, "Can we help our young readers to be masters? That's all."

Readers in the upper elementary grades meet a variety of materials which require a variety of skills and a teacher must, at this level, not only refine comprehension skills introduced in earlier grades but also expose her students to more sophisticated levels of comprehension.

Perhaps a look at several levels of comprehension and suggested procedures the teacher might use in developing competency in these levels would help to develop "masters."

In examining teaching techniques and teacher guides in primary grades, literal comprehension development is readily apparent. Children are asked to "tell" what they read; they are asked for pieces of factual information. This is good, for at the upper levels of elementary literal comprehension, it is necessary for successful performance in mathematics and science. As an example, "John is four feet tall. Does John measure four of his feet or of someone else's? Does he understand the meaning of feet?"

In another mathematics example, the reader might read the following from *Exploring Elementary Mathematics* by Keedy. "Mary had $3 to spend at the park. She wanted to take six rides that cost 35¢ each. Did she have enough money? The reader must identify the information given ($3 on hand, six rides at 35¢ each). The reader must then find the answer to "Did she have enough money?"

Consider this example: "448 city buses use 25 gallons of gasoline a day. The city pays 23¢ for a gallon of gasoline. The city pays $8.30 to clean a bus. How much does the city pay for gasoline each day?" Here the facts must be identified and then a decision must be made as to which facts are necessary.

Literal comprehension required in science might leave no room for student interpretation. Even at the elementary level, accuracy in experiments can make the difference between a successful experiment and an unsuccessful one. For example, the following simple experiment from *Science for Today and Tomorrow,* published by D. C. Heath, requires literal comprehension: "Get a piece of thread 24 inches long and tie an eraser to one end. Hold the other end still and start swinging the thread. Count the number of swings in ten seconds. Try this three times and get the average of the three trials." Certain very definite facts are given as well as very definite directions. There is no place for interpretation. The reader must be able to judge whether to apply a literal meaning or interpretive skills. He must decide whether to apply a very common meaning to one word in the sentence, one sentence in the paragraph, or one paragraph in a specific selection.

The reader must have in his storehouse of information and word meanings a variety of meanings of words. By calling upon this storehouse, the reader can then apply one of several meanings. The teacher of reading, by questions asked prior to reading, signals to the reader that he is to be alert to apply the appropriate meaning at the appropriate time.

At this point comprehension development may be no more than vocabulary development; but, at least, it is development of a variety of word meanings, phrase meanings, and subtle shadings of meanings.

Here are some examples of how a teacher might help her students develop meaning: In *Amelia Bedelia,* written by Peggy Parish and illustrated by Fritz Siebel, Amelia has the problem that many of our readers have. Amelia, the maid, believes that what is said is meant literally. This obviously causes some difficulties. Amelia's employer left her a list of jobs to do while she was out. The list read, "change the towels in the green bathroom, dust the furniture, draw the drapes when the sun comes in, put the lights out when you finish in the living room, measure two cups of rice, trim the fat before you put the steak in the icebox, and dress the chicken."

Amelia, being conscious that she had to make a good impression on her new employer, did exactly what she was told. She changed the towels; she changed them by altering their shapes with a pair of scissors. Amelia dusted the furniture; she dusted it with dusting powder that she found in the bathroom. Amelia decided that her artistic talent left something to be desired for she had difficulty drawing the drapes. The lights were put out (doors); in fact, she put them on the clothesline. She discovered in measuring the rice that a tape measure worked well. I'm sure you can imagine how she trimmed the fat on the steak and dressed the chicken.

In developing an awareness of word meanings for use in reading, why not have students illustrate literal meanings? For example: Bathroom scales—Do bathroom scales weigh bathrooms? Inchworm—Is an inchworm calibrated in one-fourth inch marks?

What about these sports terms: Kartami grabs Jones' face mask, deep center field, wing back, tight end, throw a block, the quarterback is caught in cup by a good red dog? Or, how about longhorn cheese, horsefly, or butterfly?

A class might be divided into teams of three or four students and each team would collect words or phrases which could then be presented to the opposing teams to illustrate or define. Or the original teams might compete to construct the lengthiest lists of words or phrases. The following might serve as starters: the eye of the camera, wooden ruler, the quarterback ran around his own end, stamp the letter, deliver a speech, cast a shadow, hide one's feelings, hang a picture, running water, cattails, nightmare, spelling bee, fly ball, and kneecap.

Another technique one might use in an attempt to be a master of words is to clip from the newspaper several advertisements for common products. For example, two different companies could be advertising two brands of washing machines. Have students compare the two advertisements and answer these questions: Which would you rather buy? Why? Which has more conveniences? Then, have the students strike all descriptive words from the advertisement and compare the first and second messages. How do they differ? Have students substitute antonyms for descriptive words. How is the meaning changed? Finally, each group of four or five students might design an advertisement for a common product, attempting to make their group's advertisement more enticing than the others.

All of these described activities could be used to strengthen literal comprehension and interpretive comprehension skills. Most of the activities can be open ended and can be continued as independent activities.

Although teachers in the content areas may see the importance of teaching reading skills, they often lack the necessary preservice training. Hagberg provides some examples of how content teachers can incorporate instruction in reading and related study skills within their respective subject areas.

making the right to read in the content areas a reality

betty l. hagberg
western michigan university

There is a point of view about content area reading which gives food for thought and reason for action. All subject matter requires reading, and every teacher is being admonished to teach reading in his content area although many do not know how reading is taught. The purpose of this article is to discuss the *why* of teaching reading and study skills and to suggest *how* instruction in these skills can be adapted and incorporated into daily plans. The skills suggested are common to all courses and can be taught with a minimum number of changes in classroom procedures.

content area reading—why?

Teachers of reading agree that reading is a mental process in which the reader acquires ideas; reading is not merely a word recognition exercise. Therefore, why should reading in the content areas need to be different from any reading which is done? All reading has content. If children were taught to read in social studies, science, mathematics, and literature from the very beginning of their reading instruction, they would become thinking readers regardless of the content of the material.

These three aspects of a good reading program should always

be stressed: 1) the development of basic reading skills at each grade level; 2) the integration of reading and study skills in the content areas at each successive grade level; and 3) the building and strengthening of reading interests in order to produce ever-reading students. In recent years, the prime concern of teachers has centered around the second aspect, that of integrating reading skills in the content areas at all levels of learning.

The reluctance of junior high and secondary instructors to teach content area reading usually stems from the simple fact that they have had little or no training in the teaching of reading. In the past, teachers from the primary grades through high school put students on their own in studying. They reason that pupils need to develop independent study habits before going on to the next grade. All too often students are put on their own even though they are not sufficiently prepared to cope with the material which they are expected to read. Pupils lack the study skills necessary to derive full benefits from the assigned work.

Teachers also assume that, at some other time and place, instruction in reading in the content subjects will be done. The responsibility for improving reading abilities of students gets brushed aside because teachers say that they have too much subject matter to teach and don't have time to teach reading. Teachers are ignoring the fact that reading instruction does not take place solely during that period of time traditionally set aside for the developmental reading class.

Probably the best job of reading instruction has been done at the primary level. Yet, the emphasis here has been mostly on word recognition, and getting meaning has been left until later. Primary and intermediate teachers who are usually in self-contained classrooms, as well as junior high and secondary instructors, are responsible for teaching reading in the content subjects. When challenged to teach reading at the upper levels, teachers are fearful that they will be forced to teach reading rather than subject content. Reading instruction is viewed as an added burden rather than as an integral part of effective instruction.

The crux of the problem for classroom teachers at all levels lies in the fact that they do not know how to teach reading in their content subjects. Let us look at practical and workable techniques of this particular process.

introducing the textbook

Introduce the textbook at the beginning of the course. This can be either the dynamic start which promises a successful course, or a weak beginning which turns students off. Enthusiasm encourages student interest in the course contents.

Have you ever heard a teacher present a textbook to a class in a deadly, droning, threatening, and unenthusiastic way? "Here's the book we're going to have in math this year. Take decent care of it. You will be held responsible for it as I have the number of each book and the name of the person to whom it was given." Often the teacher will add, "I don't particularly like this text but we can't afford new ones." Would that excite and interest you in the contents of that book? Teachers must be interested in their courses and chosen textbooks. They should discuss the importance of the following:

1. *Title of the text.*

2. *Author or Authors.*
   Do they appear to be authorities in their field?

3. *Copyright date.*
   Why is it important to know this fact?

4. *Table of contents.*
   How does it help determine the scope and structure of the text? The author's opinion of the relative importance of different chapters may be noted by the number of pages devoted to them.

5. *Scanning the index.*
   Indicate to students how the Index leads to specific information and definite facts while the Table of Contents gives a general overview of the material in the text.

6. *Skimming the appendix.*
   Determine what supplemental aids have been made available. Bibliographies, references, statistical tables, explanatory notes, and visual aids are often supplied.

7. *Scanning the glossary.*
   Indicate to students that the glossary is a valuable tool since it contains words and terms they need to know in order to read the text intelligently.

8. *Examining the chapters in the text.*
   What is the format of each chapter? Does the writer supply major and minor headings? What use does the writer make of maps, charts, graphs, and pictures? Explain to students why visual aids are included in a book and point out their purpose of clarifying concepts presented in the text.

previewing and studying material effectively

Students can be taught how to read for main ideas, to read for a purpose, and to make ideas their own. This can be done very effectively through the PQRST method of study, using the regular textbook for the course being taught. The P stands for *preview,* meaning to preview the book, chapter, or article, which is an excellent way of helping students to set a purpose for reading any material. If a purpose is set and a background is built before reading an assignment, the student will know what to look for while reading and will be aided in concentrating on the selection to be read. A reader who has "nothing in mind" gains little from his reading. Previewing is also an excellent way for a content teacher to introduce an assignment. Merely assigning a number of pages and directing students to read them is a very poor way in which to set a purpose for reading. The threat of a quiz adds little incentive for reading an assignment.

Previewing, or setting a purpose, is accomplished by reading the title, introduction, summary, major headings, and questions at the end of the chapter or section. The reader can learn the writer's intentions and ideas and can become aware of what the writer thinks is important.

Some books, essays, and reports lack main headings and subheadings; in this case, use topic sentences. The sentences are valuable for revealing the framework of the chapter, article, or whatever the selection might be. The reader can compose his own main headings along the page margins.

The slow, word-by-word reader especially needs to learn to use this method of previewing. The disabled reader is one of the basic concerns of all content teachers, and instructors often reach a point of desperation and give up on these students. If anyone needs to know the short cuts, it is the disabled reader. A slow reader faced with reading an entire chapter may venture through only the first three to five paragraphs and have only a small, meaningless idea of the entire assignment. By previewing a chapter the reader is given an overall view, a complete outline, and a framework to aid listening. He can learn the details through the class discussions.

The Q in PQRST indicates to the reader that the major headings are to be converted into questions.

The R directs the student to read to answer the questions. The questions may be answered in three to five points; more than this amount leads the reader into too much detail.

The S means that the answers must be stated in one's own words and not copied from the book. It is in analyzing the author's words and then synthesizing the ideas into one's own words that a clear understanding of the concept is gained.

The *T* suggests testing for mastery of the material just studied. The testing may take place immediately after the study period or at a later time as a review of the assignment. This is an excellent study method which may be introduced, with modification, as early as the third grade and can continue through college levels.

building content course vocabulary

Another study skill which is extremely important to content teachers is that of continually building technical vocabulary. Course connected vocabulary must be introduced daily to the class by defining and discussing words which are pertinent for effective reading and listening in that content subject. Students should not be left on their own to discover the words. Often, the technical words of a particular subject are not found in desk dictionaries. Therefore, students should be guided to use the glossary supplemented by class discussions of particular words. The importance of learning technical terms cannot be overstressed.

teaching selective reading techniques

Teach students the skills of skimming and scanning, two important forms of selective reading.

Skimming is the process used when a student wants to get a general idea of an article, chapter, book, or report. In a book this may be done by reading chapter titles and major headings; topic sentences may be read in skimming an article or a report.

Scanning is the process of quickly searching for a specific idea or concept. Students scan a dictionary in search of a particular word, and they may scan a chapter for a specific date, name, or event.

The content teacher will help students to study effectively by presenting *underlining* and *coding* techniques. These are especially recommended for material with much factual data.

Notetaking is an essential skill for students and is best taught by content teachers. The teachers must demonstrate on the chalkboard how students should take notes in classes and from textbooks. Notetaking can differ markedly from course to course depending on the content of the course.

improving other study skills

The preceding study procedures have been emphasized because one of the most consistent problems apparent in student failure is the lack of appropriate ways to study. Simple exposure and experimentation with study skills can avoid unnecessary failure for pupils at all levels of learning. The reading study skills just presented are common to all content areas. Other common study skills might include: how to read and follow directions in academic material, how to read test questions and write examinations, and how to prepare assignments.

Each content subject has specific reading and study skills which must be taught. Teachers cannot assume that students come to their classrooms already knowing how to read and study in that subject matter or at that particular grade level. A first grader must learn what a story problem is in mathematics. For example: "Jane and Sue were playing in the yard." Is this a problem? No, it is a statement of fact. It tells something. "Three other girls came to play with Jane and Sue." Is this a problem? No, another fact has been stated. "How many girls altogether were playing in the yard?" Is this a problem? Yes, a question has been asked that makes use of the given facts. A story problem must have two parts. One part gives facts you need to know. Another part asks the question that uses the facts. The key word, *altogether,* directs the student to the process he will use to solve the problem. Such words as *altogether* and *how many in all* give the clue to use the addition process. Words such as *solve, process,* and *addition,* must be defined, explained, and discussed with the students.

As a child progresses from grade level to grade level, questions requiring addition will be asked in many varied ways. The math teacher at each grade level will be expected to teach students how to read and solve story problems by reviewing what they have supposedly learned and by teaching the additional advanced skill to be learned at the student's present grade level. Math teachers discuss with students the special characteristics of mathematical reading. Every word and every symbol are important. The text of math is compact and calls for slow, analytical reading.

The reading of story problems involves five different processes: 1) reading the entire problem to grasp the whole idea, 2) concentrating on the questions or statements at the end which tell what to find, 3) determining how many working steps to use in getting the answer, 4) deciding what process or formula to use in working each step, and 5) pulling out the number facts to be used in working the problem.

Teaching students how to read and solve problems cannot be accomplished by putting them on their own with an assigned number of problems to be completed. The teacher must be involved by providing students with special practice in reading procedures entailed and offering assistance as difficulties arise.

In each content area at each successive grade level, the teacher needs to interact and become involved with his students every day. Children are not promoted to the next grade level because they already have the skills to master the materials at that level, but because they are ready to be instructed at that particular grade level in mathematics, science, literature, and history. It cannot be assumed that students entering sixth grade can read and complete workbook assignments on their own. The teacher must be involved in showing students how to read and follow directions and should point out the key words which will enable the students to follow directions. The teacher who aids students in this way is involved in teaching reading skills.

conclusion

Good content area teachers do not engage in assumptive teaching. They do not assume that their pupils already have the reading and study skills which are needed to function at grade level. They are involved with student learning and are aware of how and when to teach the various reading skills. These teachers are enthusiastic and interested in their subject matter. They make the "right to read" in the content areas a reality for students.

references

1. Bamman, Henry A. "Developing Reading Competencies Through Math and Science," in J. Allen Figurel (Ed.), *Reading As An Intellectual Activity,* Proceedings of the International Reading Association, 8, 1963. New York: Scholastic Magazines.
2. Carter, Homer L. J., and Dorothy J. McGinnis. *Reading: A Key to Academic Success.* Dubuque, Iowa: Wm. C. Brown, 1967.
3. Gates, Arthur I. "The Nature and Function of Reading in the Content Areas," in J. Allen Figurel (Ed.), *New Frontiers in Reading,* Proceedings of the International Reading Association, 5, 1960. New York: Scholastic Magazines.

4. Sargent, Eileen E. "Integrating Reading Skills in the Content Areas," in H. A. Robinson and E. L. Thomas (Eds.), *Fusing Reading Skills and Content*. Newark, Delaware: International Reading Association, 1969.

The Schulwitz paper highlights the creative process, offering teachers approaches to developing creative thinking in the language arts.

creativity in the elementary language arts program

bonnie smith schulwitz
central michigan university

Creativity—its definition, its significance, and its facilitation—has been a persistent, recurring issue throughout the history of education. A profound resurgence of interest in creativity is evidenced today as the pressures of our present world demand the talents of the creative mind.

toward a definition

If each of us were to define creativity, the resulting definitions would, undoubtedly, be as diverse as the multitude of creative approaches to any single problem, for creativity eludes precise, universal definition. Perhaps, it is due, in part, to the fact that the very essence of creativity is not convergence but rather divergence. Guilford's account (1) of the nature of creative thinking includes this characteristic of divergent thinking, which he defines as the ability to think in different directions. It is the kind of thinking that produces a variety of responses instead of one single correct response. According to Guilford, divergent thinking is characterized by originality, flexibility, and fluency. In this context, creativity is considered to be a process of divergent thought which may be developed in children and utilized by them in many different situations.

some assumptions

It is this interpretation of creativity which forms the theoretical perspective for this discussion. In addition, three assumptions contribute to the perspective. Lytton (3) suggests the first assumption in his book, *Creativity and Education.* He asserts that creative potential exists in every human being, and its development is subject to the experiences and human encounters of one's life. It is this potential to which Rogers (4) speaks when he states, "The mainspring of creativity appears to be the same tendency which we discover so deeply as the curative force in psychotherapy—man's tendency to actualize himself, to become his potentialities."

The second assumption is that creativity can manifest itself in many diverse activities. One need only to watch a child at play to observe his creative discovery of an original way to go down a slide or even up a slide! Or a teacher can be creative in what otherwise might be considered by some to be a most mundane teaching responsibility—collecting the milk money.

Believing that creative potentialities exist within each unique individual and believing that they may be revealed in any endeavor leads to the third assumption that we, as teachers, must adopt an active role in developing these potentialities and must provide opportunities for their expression. It is the purpose of this paper to explore the means by which teachers can facilitate the development of creativity in children and to illustrate instructional strategies designed to develop creative thinking in the elementary language arts program.

facilitating the development of creativity

How can teachers set conditions for a creative climate which fosters the growth of creativity? One way may be called "creating the creative spirit." The "Fable of the Four Mice" illustrates this step.

Once upon a time there were four mice who lived in a barn. One mouse lived high up in the barn, one mouse lived at the back of the barn, one mouse lived in a wall on one side of the barn, and one mouse lived near the front door of the barn. Now, sometimes High Mouse (the one who lived high up in the barn) heard strange noises down below him. Every time he heard these noises he would look down through a knothole in the floor. That is how he found out that things that say "Moo" look like cows as viewed from above; things that say "Hee Haw" look like donkeys as viewed from above; and things that say "Oink, Oink" look like pigs viewed this way. Now Back Mouse, (who lived at the back of the barn) heard strange noises, too. Every time he heard these noises he would look out to see what made them. And that is how Back Mouse found out that things that say "Moo" look like cows as viewed from the back; things that say "Hee Haw" look like donkeys as viewed from the back; and things that say "Oink, Oink" look like pigs as viewed from the back. Side Mouse lived in a wall at one side of the barn. When he heard strange noises, he would peek out to see what made them. And that is how he found out that things that say "Moo," "Hee Haw," and "Oink, Oink" look like cows, donkeys, and pigs as viewed from the side. Front Mouse lived near the front door. When he heard the strange noises, he would peek out too. That is how he found out that things that say, "Moo" and "Hee Haw" and "Oink, Oink" look like cows, donkeys, and pigs from a front view. Now, one day all of the mice heard a new noise that went, "Meow." They scurried into the storeroom where the thing that said "Meow" couldn't get in. All of a sudden the sound came again. They stopped and looked and that is the way they all found out that things that say "Meow" look like cats would look from the front. Then suddenly, the thing turned and walked along the window sill. Then they found out that things that say "Meow" can look like cats would look from the side. Just then, the thing turned and walked away so they found it can look like a cat would look from the back. When the thing jumped down to the floor below, they found out, as they looked through a crack in the floor, that it can look like a cat would look from the top. And so it was that High Mouse, Front Mouse, Side Mouse, and Back Mouse all found out something else. They found out that one thing can look many different ways —as many different ways as there are perspectives from which to look at it. (Author Unknown)

How beautifully this little fable serves as our classroom model in creating a climate for accepting the divergence, the individuality, the uniqueness of each child's perceptions. In retelling it to children, let us go a step beyond acceptance to the encouragement of individuality.

Teachers equipped with the power of positive teaching have discovered another way to establish a creative spirit. They convey positive expectations to the children. Then the children, imbued with the "I can" feeling, fulfill these expectations. Art Combs offers some principles to follow in this responsibility. He states, "If you tell a child a task is easy and he can't do it, how incapable you have made the child feel! If you tell him it is easy and he can do it, you've robbed the child of some of the glory of accomplishment when he does it. But, if you tell him it is hard but you believe he can do it, you've conveyed your faith in his ability, while he enjoys the marvelous sense of success at having achieved a difficult task." The teacher who can implement this philosophy is the teacher who knows well what Stephens (5) means: "I have learned that the head does not hear anything until the heart has listened, and what the heart knows today, the head will understand tomorrow."

developing creative thinking in the language arts

What specific instructional strategies can elementary teachers employ to encourage creativity in the elementary language arts? The following suggestions relate to three major topics: 1) mind-expanding approaches, 2) mind-expanding activities, and 3) mind-expanding materials.

1. Approaches
   a. Approach creative expression in speaking, reading, writing, and acting as each child's expression of his own unique impression. Encourage the divergent viewpoint, value individuality, and praise originality.
   b. Develop creative expression by providing opportunities for it in speaking, reading, writing, and acting out.
   c. Encourage creative interpretation in language arts activities by the use of mind-expanding questions. Going beyond the literal, categorical questions to those that ask, "How many different ways can you . . . ?" "Can you think of all the things that could happen . . . ?" "What do *you* think about this situation?"
   d. Be aware of the dangers of subjective evaluation. A seventeen-year-old ghetto student described an incident which emphasizes this point. "It all started five years ago in the sixth grade. The teacher gave us a writing assignment to do and I was the first one finished so I thought that I would have some fun. So I drew a picture of a man committing suicide and I wrote that the man said that he was going to kill himself. And my teacher saw it and thought that I was going to kill myself. She gave it to the principal and the principal gave it to my doctor and he gave it to a psychiatrist up in New Jersey and the psychiatrist said that I was mentally disturbed" (2).
2. Activities
   a. Originality in thinking can be developed by having children pantomime an activity. Oral language or written language can then be developed by individual interpretation of the pantomime.

132   *Developing Creative Thinking*

b. Flexibility in thinking can be developed by having the children think up uses for objects, improvements for things in our environment, or consequences for a situation: "List all the consequences that would happen if. . . ."
c. Associational fluency can be developed utilizing the brainstorming technique with words as children say or write synonyms or antonyms.
3. Materials
a. Search for children's books which are mind-expanding. Lionni's *Little Blue and Little Yellow* and Yashima's *Seashore Story* are illustrative. Picard's *One is One* and Ferra's *Twelve People is Not a Dozen* emphasize respect for individuality.
b. Utilize the materials in a way which encourages creative divergent thinking. After reading a story, the child should be encouraged to incorporate his own interpretation, feeling, and ending.

Finally, be attuned to seeing the seed of creative potential in the soul of each child. Warm it, water it, feed it, nurture it with love and acceptance, for our task is to cultivate creativity for the benefit of the world today as well as tomorrow.

references

1. Guilford, J. P. "Creativity," *American Psychologist,* 5 (1950).
2. Joseph, Stephen M. *The Me Nobody Knows.* New York: Avon Books, 1969.
3. Lytton, Hugh. *Creativity and Education.* New York: Schocken Books, 1972.
4. Rogers, Carl R. "Toward a Theory of Creativity," in Harold H. Anderson (Ed.), *Creativity and Its Cultivation.* New York: Harper and Brothers, 1959.
5. Stephens, James. *The Crock of Gold: Irish Folktales.* New York: Macmillan.

Murray's creative approaches, designed to strengthen reading through the study of writing, expand the dimension of integrated language arts instruction. He offers many practical ideas so teachers may adopt his "Write to Read" approach.

write to read: creative writing in the reading program

donald m. murray
university of new hampshire

In the reading or literature program, the students study finished writing. Their job is to understand what the writer has said and to appreciate how he has said it. In the writing program, the students study unfinished writing. They read writing-in-process to help themselves or others discover what they have to say and how to communicate it effectively.

Reading writing-in-process is different from the reading we normally teach in elementary through graduate school. It is, however, a careful and exciting kind of reading which can make the student a more effective reader of finished or published writing.

The student of writing learns by experiencing the stages of prewriting, writing, and rewriting through which the writer discovers what he has to say. Using language as a tool of personal exploration, the student begins to see and understand his world as he never has before. Previously, the student thought of writing as a product, what was done; now he sees it as a process, what can be done.

The student also begins to realize that writing is never really finished. He understands Paul Valery, who said, "A poem is never finished, it is only abandoned." Writing is an evolving process of understanding.

Without realizing it, the student writer becomes a sophisticated and skillful reader. He reads what is on the page a dozen times—maybe a dozen times a dozen—to make sure each word is right, to be certain that the line of sentences leads toward his intended meaning. This process isn't boring, for the student often discovers what he didn't know he knew.

In this way the student learns to read as a writer, as one who sees the possibilities behind each line. It is worth noting his experience in reading is achieved through three meaningful writing tasks:

1. The student reads and rereads his own page to discover what he means and how he can communicate it effectively.
2. The student reads classmates' papers (and hopefully the teacher's) in workshop sessions to help them see how their papers might be written with greater clarity or grace.
3. The student reads published writers to see how they have done what he is trying to do.

Note that all this reading has a specific purpose, and in each case the student is using language with care and concern. The student discovers that choices of language are important and that one word can carry the reader toward the truth while another word can betray him.

This insider's view of how the writer reads can be made available to the student of reading or literature, if both teacher and student realize that writing doesn't mysteriously happen to the author. The author plans and prepares, considers and reconsiders, puts words in and takes words out, experiments, builds, and writes. The writer may make a thousand decisions on a single page, and each time he rereads that page he clicks through those decisions and reviews them.

Consider this simple situation. The writer has to choose a verb to describe what the character is doing. He puts down, "Robert weeps." Think of all the words he has to know and reject to select that one. Some of the words which could have been used include cries, moans, sniffles, sobs, whimpers, wails, and screams. The writer's burden is to pick the word which is right and which is accurate for the character and the situation. He has to consider the word in relation to other words as well as its connotation and denotation. Has it been used too many times? Should it be saved for another time? There are many choices and once the final word has been chosen, the writer understands the character better than before.

I have found this process of choice and discovery essential to writing fiction, nonfiction, and poetry. To the writer there is no such thing as creative writing and functional writing; there is only bad writing and good writing, and good writing is the result of making careful, honest decisions during the writing process. Most of these decisions come after a careful rereading of a draft.

The reading teacher and his students must understand that writing is not so much a matter of magic as of craft. The poet rarely is inspired to toss off easy lines combining truth and beauty. Listen to writers talk of how they reread and rewrite.

Poet and novelist, James Dickey:
"It takes an awful lot of time for me to write anything. I have endless drafts, one after another; and I try out 50, 75, or a hundred variations on a single line sometimes. I work on the process of refining low-grade ore. I get maybe a couple of nuggets of gold out of 50 tons of dirt. It is tough for me. No, I am not inspired."

Philosopher and novelist, William Gass:
"I work not by writing but by rewriting. Each sentence has many drafts. Eventually there is a paragraph. This gets many drafts. Eventually there is a page. This gets many drafts."

Poet and novelist, Robert Graves:
"I wrote it [*The White Goddess*] in six weeks. It took me ten years to revise it."

Poet, Ann Sexton:
"I've revised as much as three hundred times on one lyric poem."

Writer of short stories and children's books, Roald Dahl:
"By the time I am nearing the end of a story, the first part will have been reread and altered and corrected at least one hundred and fifty times."

Novelist, Gustav Flaubert:
"Whatever the thing you wish to say, there is but one word to express it, but one verb to give it movement, but one adjective to qualify it; you must seek until you find this noun, this verb, this adjective."

Once the student begins to appreciate and share the writer's search to discover what has to be said, he begins to see that all published writers engaged in an exploration can be second-guessed and understood. The student writer begins to appreciate writing in a new way, and reads to comprehend the spectrum of choices the writer faced. Eight of the principal decisions a writer has to make are:

1. *Subject.* A writer at work makes choices which keep narrowing the subject. As the subject is limited, space is gained to develop it adequately.

2. *Attitude.* The writer develops an attitude toward the subject through writing about it. A point of view evolves which may be stated directly to the reader or may be hidden, but it is there and is a factor in all the writer's choices of craft.

3. *Form.* The writer chooses a form or genre which will carry his meaning to his audience. Writing forms are not rigid, they stretch, expand, and contract, but they do have functional limits which influence many writing decisions.

4. *Audience.* The writer will not communicate effectively unless he keeps an eye on his audience to make sure that everything he has to say is said as clearly and simply as possible. He must read his own copy as a stranger.

5. *Documentation.* The writer writes with information, and thus should be able to select the most effective pieces of documentation from an abundance of details as the piece is developed. Information is chosen which will support and communicate what the writer has to say.

6. *Voice.* The writer listens to his own voice, making adjustments in language until his voice is consistent and appropriate. A writer should be an individual speaking to an individual.

7. *Structure.* The writer builds writing. He creates order out of chaos and constructs what he has to say so that the reader can see its significance.

8. *Language.* All writing comes down to choosing words which are honest, accurate, and graceful. The writer considers and reconsiders changes, moves about, qualifies, and complicates his language until he understands what he has to say, so that a reader may also understand. The writer's words are the tools utilized to discover his meaning.

The student reader should see all those potential editorial decisions and then consciously put himself at the writer's desk so that he can imagine the process of selection—conscious or subconscious—through which the writer created the final draft. Some of the questions which should be asked of the page are:

- What other way could the writer have done this?
- Why did the writer make this choice?
- How did the writer make it work this way?
- What are some of the chances the writer took in doing it this way?

Those questions can and should be asked of any piece of writing. Reading activities such as the following can help your students read as a writer:

1. Study texts which reproduce early and final versions of writers' manuscripts to show the choices famous writers have made. Some of these books are: *The Poet's Craft* by A. F. Scott, *Creative Writing and Rewriting* by John Juehl, *Word for Word* and *Writing With Care* by Wallace Hildick, *Visions and Revisions* by Barry Wallenstein, and *Poems in Process* by Phyllis Bartlett.

2. In order to legitimize the essential process of rewriting and revision through which the writer discovers his meaning, use phonograph records which perform early drafts of composers' famous works, reproduction of artists' sketchbooks, or the accounts of scientific discoveries.

3. Have your students write variations of a paragraph or page from a famous writer and consciously change the tone, audience, structure, and language. Reproduce the versions without identifying who wrote them, and let the class discuss which draft is more effective. Remember, they don't have to guess the published version. The author's writing was in process too; what he published may not be the best version.

4. Have your students cut a piece of writing to a quarter of its original length to get an interior view of what the writer did.

5. Take an important sentence from a published writer and have a contest to see how many different ways that sentence can be rewritten.

6. Encourage students to write adaptations of a piece of fiction for a movie, play, or television series as a way of reexamining what the writer did.

7. Compare the published copy of a well-known play or movie with the original book version.

8. Pick the writers with whom your students are most familiar, and have them write paragraphs in the voices of different writers such as Hemingway, Faulkner, Steinbeck, Salinger, and Mailer.

9. Clip a story on a significant news event from many newspapers and magazines to see how the same facts may be handled differently. Have some of your students report on how the same event was covered on radio and television.

10. Invite a local author to come to class. Ask the author if he would be willing to show manuscript drafts of a single page or paragraph so that the class could see the choices he made. Remember, this writer may be a judge or a real-estate salesman known for writing interesting ads. The writer is a person who uses language with care.

11. Give identical facts to the class, or have them observe the same place, person, or event. Have them write a paragraph; compare the different versions.

12. Have students write a short scene in different genres—a few pages from a play, novel, poem, newspaper story, or history book.

13. Have students take broad subjects and consciously limit them by narrowing them down through a dozen steps. They could, for example, begin with paragraphs about a town and then move through the neighborhood to one house and then to one room. Notice the choices the writers have to make at each stage.

14. Take the lead, the first ten lines or so, of a piece of writing and rewrite it for various magazines (such as *Time, New Yorker, Reader's Digest,* and *Saturday Review*).

15. Encourage your students to read aloud, one after another, a piece of writing to show how oral interpretation can change the emphasis of the piece.

16. Have your students rewrite a story, making a different person the hero or heroine.

17. Have your students write a story from a different point of view, or switch from third person to first person or vice versa.

18. Have your students write a story as if it took place in a different age or a different locale.

19. Have your students rewrite a favorite story for a much younger audience.

20. Have your students translate from a foreign language or into a made-up language so that they can understand this process of choice.

21. Have your students write a news story on a lab report, a political speech, or a law.

22. Have your students write a speech which illustrates the different choices of language which are made when a piece of writing is to be spoken rather than read.

These are just a few of the ways your class can read to discover the choices a writer makes. Have your students design their own exercises to explore the world of possibility which lies behind each piece of writing.

As your students begin to see that writing was the product of choice, they will begin to see the drafts which lie behind each published page and they will read with greater care, understanding, and appreciation.

MURRAY

A six-pronged program for teaching literature in the elementary school is outlined, illustrated, and evaluated in terms of the values to children. The major focus is on the ways literature may be integrated into the total curriculum.

approaches to the use of literature in the reading program

helen huus
university of missouri

This paper appraises some of the approaches currently labeled "literature teaching," and then it describes a total program. The literature program is here defined as a planned program of teaching that uses books of recognized quality to achieve the following objectives: enjoyment (including imagination stretching); acquaintance with the literary heritage; an understanding of what constitutes literature; application of literature in personal living; and the ability to evaluate, appreciate, and develop personal tastes. By *literature* is meant the writing kept alive through time by its beauty of style or thought—writing that is artistic in form and which appeals to the emotions. Literature worthy of the designation has layers of depth that allow the selection to be reread countless times, and each rereading uncovers meanings hitherto unrecognized or forgotten. Gerber maintains that literature is "written for people to read; it is designed to evoke feeling and belief and not just understanding and not just a sense of form" (2). *Literature for children* means classical or contemporary writing of such quality that children can understand what is read or heard.

140

program approaches

The literature program is distinct from the teaching of reading, yet is tightly interwoven with it. Students must learn how to read before they can read independently; although, ideally, the literature program need not wait until this phenomenon occurs. Learning begins as soon as the child is born. Mothers sing lullabies, recite verses, and play patty-cake before infants can make both hands meet, and story reading continues in preschool years when parents or baby sitters take the time.

The planned literature program, however, begins with school and usually is approached in six different ways in various combinations: 1) free reading by children, 2) reading aloud to children, 3) guided and supplementary reading, 4) topical units, 5) creative sharing, and 6) a combined program that includes literature teaching.

free reading

A literature program of free reading is variously organized, but it usually provides a certain amount of time each week for students to read books of their own choosing. Pupils are usually not free *not* to read, but they are free to read what they wish and supposedly what they can—even comic books, series like Nancy Drew or The Hardy Boys, and maybe *Mad Magazine!*

Last year one elementary school gained quite a reputation as "A Reading School." Each afternoon after lunch, "Please Do Not Disturb" signs were hung on every door to inform anyone who came that a reading period was in progress. During this half hour, everyone in the building read: the students, the teachers, the principal and his secretary, and the janitor!

Free reading does have a place in the literature program. It allows pupils to read what they wish, to not finish every book they start, to select material considered by interested adults to be too difficult or too easy for them, and to pursue one topic relentlessly.

However, free reading has disadvantages, even when it is only part of a total literature program. The approach assumes that pupils have a wide range of choices available on many topics of varying levels of difficulty so that they can find what they want to read and be able to read it. This is not always the case. In addition, some pupils may stay too long on one level and fail to progress to books of greater depth; some may read superficially and be satisfied with only cursorily following a story plot or with merely looking at pictures; and others may have difficulty in choosing books from those available and thus may waste their time. The free reading done at home has similar advantages and disadvantages, provided the reader has a suitable place to read.

If free reading is only one prong of a total program, it can contribute by capturing and extending the readers' interests and by easing pupils into a more structured approach.

reading aloud

In some schools, the only literature offered for oral reading is that presented during the ten- or fifteen-minute period set aside for the teacher or a student to read aloud to the class. The material may consist of short stories, poetry, or a chapter-a-day from a longer book.

When the reader is well prepared and when the book is chosen with the total class in mind, such oral reading is often interesting and enjoyable. Furthermore, since pupils are not doing the reading for themselves, they have no responsibility other than listening; they can hear books with a vocabulary and language structure beyond their current competencies, and being unhampered by problems of reading, they can focus on actions and ideas; they can hear the beauty of the language as it sounds; and they can listen to stories that they ordinarily might miss. Some pupils would shun poetry completely, and few boys today are likely to pick out *Alice in Wonderland* for their free reading, although one sixth grade boy did admit to reading *Little Women* because he had heard it was a good book.

On the other hand, when someone reads aloud, pupils may be relatively passive and thus profit less from the experience than they would have if they had read the book themselves. Books selected for reading aloud can take into account the interests of a majority of the students or the known interests of a given age group, but such books may fail to capture the interest of other individuals. Regardless of age, those who have not learned to read are dependent upon those who can read. For some pupils, a pressure to learn to read can be generated because they want so much to read for themselves a story they enjoyed hearing; other pupils may be completely satisfied to continue their dependency and simply listen. In any case, listening to fine stories and poems read well orally is another important prong of the program for literature and is one way children become acquainted with their literary heritage.

Storytelling can be placed in the same category as reading aloud, for it has most of the same advantages and disadvantages. The fact that a storyteller usually has no book between himself and the listener is often cited as the crucial contribution. However, a storyteller who feels the responsibility of fidelity to the author's composition may still wish to have the book as a prompter, if needed.

Storytelling falls short as literature when the teller takes great liberties with the vocabulary and syntax of an author's writing and gives pupils, at best, a poor substitute that happens to be the teller's personal version of the story. It is also a disadvantage when the storyteller fails to submerge his own personality in favor of the work.

A library story hour is subject to the same pitfalls, for even though pupils hear a story read or told, the literary experience depends upon the quality of the selection, the authenticity of the rendition, and the attention to elements constituting literature. Unless the latter is present, pupils have a pleasant and comfortable time hearing old favorites and getting acquainted with new stories, but they may not be progressing in their literature learning.

guided and supplementary reading

Guided reading and supplementary reading refute some of the criticisms leveled at free reading. In the guided program, students are given help in selecting the books they wish to read, with consideration given to a variety of types and topics and to levels of quality and difficulty. Guidance is apparent when librarians color-code books for difficulty or place books on shelves by topic and grade level. Just making a book available in the library, classroom, or at home is another subtle way of channeling the pupils' choices.

More pointed guidance is given in school subjects when additional readings are recommended on the topic studied. Alert teachers note possibilities before the topic is initiated and procure the recommended books so that they are available at the outset. Library books enhance the regularly assigned lessons by expanding and explaining ideas which a textbook, of necessity, merely generalizes. Biographies can bring to life persons who are mentioned only briefly in a line of text. Whole eras, countries, or concepts can be illustrated through narration, drama, poetry, fiction, and pictures.

However, not all supplementary reading can be classed as literature for some informational books are trite, stilted, made-to-order books devised to reach a ready market. In contrast to such books are the beautifully written factual accounts like the animal stories of Mary and Conrad Buff or Jean George; the biographies of James Daugherty or Jean Lee Latham; the historical fiction of Elizabeth Janet Gray or

Rosemary Sutcliff; or the almost-true accounts of Laura Ingalls Wilder, Kate Seredy, and Carol Ryrie Brink. While fewer literary books on useful topics serve as supplementary reading materials in subject areas, the distinction between quality writing and reportorial recitation must be recognized.

Relating literature to other school subjects serves to reinforce both and helps pupils realize the range of style possible when dealing with varied topics such as elephants, snow, frontier life, or ancient Peru. Literature may fire a student's imagination for far away places or unresearched areas and may have a lasting influence on his vocational choice or avocational pursuits. The background pupils acquire through well-written informational books stands them in good stead later, and the experience with factual books of quality helps acquaint students with literary elements—irrespective of topic—which may provide motivation for further, more advanced reading about peoples, places, and things. Supplementary reading, then, has a place as another prong in the total literature program.

topical units

The approach to literature that utilizes units on a topic or subject, a type of work, or the style of writing also is related to supplementary reading.

Topics like "People of Other Lands," "The Oregon Trail," "The City," "Animals that Live in the Sea," "Plants that Move," "Machines," and "The First Thanksgiving" are familiar to teachers. In some classrooms, literature is organized around calendar topics—"September," "Fall," "Halloween," "Book Week," "Veterans' Day," "Thanksgiving," and so on through the year.

A topic like "Spring" can lead in several directions. One might focus on "Growing Things," starting out with plants and animals and promoting books such as *Maple Tree* by Millicent Selsam, *Lookout for the Forest* by Glenn Blough, and *Green is for Growing* by Winifred and Cecil Lubell. "Animals and How They Grow" could be introduced through Holling Clancy Holling's *Pagoo* which tells of the life of a hermit crab, and Herbert Zim's books that follow life cycles in *Monkeys, Elephants, Rabbits,* and *The Great Whales*. Reptiles could be introduced through Robert McClung's dramatic *Buzztail,* the story of a rattlesnake, as well as John Hoke's *First Book of Snakes* and Barbara Brenner's *A Snake Lover's Diary*. Books about birds, insects, and human beings could be added as the topic expands and as pupils are led to see similarities among all the growing things which struggle for survival.

Other topics comparing and contrasting older classics like *Little Women* and *Tom Sawyer* with modern counterparts like *Up a Road Slowly, Island of the Blue Dolphins, It's Like This, Cat,* and *Henry Reed, Inc.* provide the basis for a literature unit where relationships between parents and children, siblings, peers, or sexes can be discussed.

Young children might compare contemporary editions of Mother Goose illustrated by Tasha Tudor, Brian Wildsmith, Philip Reed, Marguerite de Angeli, and Harold Jones with classical editions illustrated by Kate Greenaway, Randolph Caldecott, Walter Crane, L. Leslie Brooke, and Blanche Fisher Wright. Pupils can note the inclusiveness of the collection, versions used, color, action, period depicted, and placement of illustrations in relation to the verses.

Types of literary works might be featured, such as biography, folk and fairy tales (which could be coupled with other topics such as France, Japan, or Brazil), tall tales, poetry, plays (though these are few for the elementary school), myths, hero tales, and picture books.

"American Tall Tales" might be chosen as pupils read and compare the exploits of John Henry, Paul Bunyan, Pecos Bill, Joe Magarac, Febold Feboldson, Mike Fink, Tony Beaver, Stormalong the Sailor, and other half-true heroes such as Davy Crockett, Johnny Appleseed, and perhaps Daniel Boone and Buffalo Bill. Anne Malcolmson's *Yankee Doodle's Cousins* still gives a fine overview of these characters and can easily be followed by books about each individual.

Style is another common denominator for a topical unit, and books containing various types of humor—exaggeration or funny characters—could be compared. Various figures of speech, realistic conversations, lifelike portrayals of characters, or variations in levels of language are other dimensions of style to be noted and discussed.

For illustration, suppose a unit or lesson focuses on the simile as a figure of speech. The teacher first might explain that unknown objects and ideas can be made real and understandable when compared to something the reader already knows. Borten's *Do You See What I See?* (1) contains similes on nearly every page. In this book the author discusses lines, shapes, and colors. Note how her similes in these descriptions relate both to content and to feeling:

Lines can bend in a curved way, too. A curved line is like a swan, full of beauty and grace. It can rise and curl slowly, as lazy as smoke. It can twirl like a dancer, or flow and swirl like water in a stream full of speckled fish.

A circle is a "shape"—a merry, cherry shape. It can roll like a ball, or float like a bubble, or turn like a ferris wheel. It can be calm as the moon, as gentle as a curled-up kitten, or as fat and jolly as Santa Claus.

Different colors make us feel different ways, just as lines and shapes do. Red is hot like a crackling fire, and blue is cold like a mountain stream.

Yellow is warm like the sun's rays, and green is as cool as a crisp leaf of lettuce.

Poetry, too, contains pictures. Tippet's poem, "The Park" (4), describes the lights that shine "as bright and still/ As dandelions/ On a hill." Kuskin's snake "moved like a ribbon/Silent as snow," (3) and Lewis' trumpet "honks and it whistles/ It roars like lion/ With a wheezing huffing hum" (3). Children understand the idea and later can make their own comparisons and eventually learn the term.

According to the National Assessment of Educational Progress reports on literature, more than half of the 9- and 13-year-olds expressed personal involvement with the literary works and made a value judgment or evaluation of them. At most, about a third of these age groups were able to analyze, describe, and interpret the works. Although more than half of these pupils evaluated the material, apparently they were unable to support their evaluations through analysis and interpretation. These pupils may not know how to analyze and interpret literary works. The types of analyses and interpretations expected may be beyond the mental capacities of certain age groups; some pupils may lack the experiential background necessary for interpretation; and some may lack the vocabulary to express ideas they recognize but cannot verbalize.

If the National Assessment test appraises the objectives accepted for literature teaching, then the implication for schools is clear: Pupils need help in supporting their value judgments of the worth and in finding the meanings of the materials they read.

Topical units or lessons have the advantage of focusing on a common thread, allowing pupils to see how various authors approach similar ideas or problems. Pupils can make comparisons and contrasts and begin to discern levels of quality among works of comparable content, genre, or style. Eventually, the earmarks of quality are identified, and students improve in their ability to evaluate. Since a class or a group of students usually works together on a topical unit, opportunities for discussion, interchange, and sharing of ideas are possible, and a teacher can structure the lessons to provide continuity and coverage. Also, students are introduced to topics and ideas that they might not consciously seek out independently, thus providing them with a fuller, richer literary experience than if left completely to their own devices.

Disadvantages of a topical-unit approach include the problem of finding topics that appeal equally to all members of the group and of obtaining adequate material of quality on a variety of different reading levels for these topics. Additional difficulties can occur in organizing and synchronizing the various activities, especially if more than one topic is selected and several groups are working simultaneously. Since individual choices would be restricted within the range of topics treated, students might also be less likely to carry over their reading into out-of-school life. Topical teaching could become routine and humdrum, though this is more a fault of poor use of the plan than of the plan itself. For many programs, units form the crux of literature teaching per se and are the central core around which other aspects cluster.

creative sharing

In some classrooms, including those at university level, the study of literature for children is approached as a vehicle for creative sharing through oral reading and storytelling; through writing compositions, original stories, critiques, and analyses; or through art activities like modeling, painting, cutting, and pasting. In this approach, discussions, choral readings, reports and reviews, dramatizations, puppet shows, pantomimes, charades and other games, murals, dioramas, overhead projection, slides, filmstrips, tapes, and records abound during the literature period.

The chief advantages of using such activities as an approach to literature are the obvious interest generated in the children and their chance to share the products with other groups and classes, parents, and casual visitors. Such tangible evidence relating to books can also serve as a means of evaluating pupils' understanding of their reading, at least on a superficial level, for literal interpretation is usually necessary to complete most of the projects developed.

There is danger, however, that creative activity may replace the literature itself, and the time allocated for reading may be usurped for production. Similarly, evaluation may become restricted to creative output and may be diverted from aspects of language and feeling to skill with paint and paper. While creative arts and literature complement each other very well, the art period can capitalize upon ideas gained from literature, and each activity may be given its place in the weekly schedule.

a total program

The learning of literature—its content, style, interpretation, emotional overtones, quality, and humanness—requires a total program that incorporates the aforementioned approaches into a flexible, overall plan. Such a plan makes provision for free reading, listening to stories and poetry read aloud, utilizing library books to supplement the content subjects, reading at home, focusing on a topical unit, learning about elements that constitute literature, and creatively sharing enjoyable books and poems. But the total program should also provide pupils with opportunities to achieve objectives at progressively higher levels as they read literature of increasing complexity and depth.

A structured program need not necessarily be formal or restricted. A teacher who recognizes and accepts the objectives of literature teaching, who knows the materials and can help pupils reach the objectives, can plan lessons that, to a casual observer, may seem to be very freewheeling in their execution. Once the lesson or series of lessons has been thought through, the teacher is free to teach a lesson as planned or to depart from it as the situation demands. What is constant is the conscious movement forward toward achieving the goals and a knowledge of what to do to create this forward movement. The real test, perhaps, will not come until the pupil leaves school and enters the working world where other pressures prevail for his time, energy, and attention.

conclusion

This discussion on approaches to literature in the elementary school has focused on the ways in which literature teaching is included in the ongoing activities of the school program. The content, activities, and evaluation of such a program have not been treated; obviously, attention must be given to the selection of concepts and content, then to the materials and activities that are utilized to obtain the objectives, and, finally, to the evaluation program that uncovers the achievement of the pupils and the strengths and weaknesses of the program.

Yet, until proven wrong, teachers must assume that teaching

literature does have lasting positive effects. The challenge is to help each student enjoy good books, improve his taste, and become acutely aware of the way literature enhances his living, enriches his experience, and sharpens his insights into the very humanity of man. A total program of literature has a chance to succeed in meeting the challenge.

references

1. Borten, Helen. *Do You See What I See?* New York: Abelard-Schuman, 1959.
2. "English Teachers Commend Free Response Exercises in Literature Assessment," *Newsletter* of the National Assessment of Educational Progress, 6 (February 1973), 4.
3. Kuskin, Karla. *In the Middle of the Trees.* New York: Harper & Row, 1958.
4. Tippett, James. "The Park," from *I Live in the City.* New York: Harper & Row, 1927, 1955.

Painter demonstrates that literature can be a valuable tool in developing reading skills.

literature develops reading skills

helen painter
kent state university

Those of us who work with children and books know the great satisfaction that exists when the two become inseparable. A book must have a reader, obviously, if its content is to become alive; a child must have books in order to grow into a feeling, perceptive, educated person.

The topic, "Literature Develops Reading Skills," calls for many basic viewpoints, which will be explored here. As a final part of this presentation, a few specific books will be used to illustrate particular skills.

underlying concepts

Perhaps the most important point as we study the topic is to state a philosophy regarding literature as a tool for teaching reading skills. For teaching a child beginning reading, this writer does not conceive of the frequently used stories of many basal readers as being literature. Similarly, the majority of articles on teaching the child beginning reading should not be categorized as literature. Such a position does not negate the value of such stories or articles. A primer or first reader is designed to present vocabulary and ideas in a simple, brief manner intended to assure success for the beginner as he tries to decode the symbols of the printed page. Similarly, articles on how to teach reading have merit in disseminating research results, theories, or practices. They are technical writings peculiar to a field. They are seldom, if ever, literature.

What is literature? Literature is that body of poetry, folklore, realism, and fantasy which has literary merit. It calls for power in the use of words, action that leads to a well-knit plot, a strong theme that presents a basic idea or truth, and realistic characters (even in fantasy) that seem to live and breathe. An author's knowledge of literary form is evident to the critic, and some wisdom evolves from the theme. The material should have interest and appeal; it should be an enjoyment to the reader.

Does children's literature possess such literary merit? Can we apply criteria of merit to it as we would to adult literature? Of course. Let us take as an example Wanda Gag's *Millions of Cats* (2), a classic tale which we all know. The motive is clear: the very old woman wants a cat because she is lonely. The very old man goes to get her one. His encounter with the cats, his human predicament of being unable to choose one from so many, and his decision to take all of them—yes, even "millions and billions and trillions of cats"—are narrated in simple, clear language. The child's awareness of the impossibly great number for anyone to take care of is shown most lucidly in two quick episodes: one drink by each cat and the water disappears; one bite of grass and the hillside is bare. Quickly the end of the story comes, the denouement, when, in the decision to keep only the prettiest, the cats fight over which is most beautiful and one scraggly cat survives. Do children believe the suggestion that the cats ate each other? Do they find that solution humorous? Or do they speculate about it? It really makes no difference, for they enjoy and think about the story. Is the surviving cat the most beautiful of all? Indeed, with love and care it became beautiful, and "I ought to know," the old man says, "because I've seen hundreds of cats, thousands of cats, millions and billions and trillions of cats." There is a moral here, of course, in the fight among the conceited and in the blossoming of something through love. It is a succinct make-believe story that is well organized and developed, full of action, and splendidly worded. It possesses literary merit as well as some entrancing illustrations. The reader or listener is involved.

Such literature may be beyond the ability of the beginning reader to read for himself, though he gains from the adult's reading it to him. Because the child lacks sufficient knowledge in phonics, word structure, and vocabulary, many teachers have turned to using the basal materials in building reading skills. The actual foundation of the program, therefore, is a pedestrian prose rather than literature. Skills are thought to take precedence over the material. Goodman (3) insists that we have been teaching reading as a set of skills to be mastered, rather than as a language process. Regardless, literature too often becomes supplementary and is used only when a teacher can and will work it into the program.

On the other hand, we have many teachers who use a total individualized approach with the beginner. In such a case children's literature becomes the basic material. Skill building is done as needed by the alert teacher with individual children or in small groups. With its emphasis on total child development, the approach has been concerned not merely with reading but with interest in and attitude toward reading. One negative criticism has dealt with skill development and the need of teacher competency in stimulating child growth in this development. While beginning reading is generally considered the most difficult place for an individualized reading program to start, some teachers have successfully used experiences and activities of children to develop charts and books of their own dictated stories and these have served as the base for skill building. They lead toward simple, published books at the appropriate reading level.

No one could quarrel with the need to build basic skills in the reading program. Usually the skills need to be taught, even to the exceptionally capable child. Time and materials are needed for introducing and consolidating such training. Literature, also, must be a part of the program. It exposes children to outstanding writing and to great truths and ideas. Through widened knowledge, sharpened sensitivity, and expanded emotions, an individual is helped to be a better person. The problem for the teacher is simply to provide for this betterment in the reading program. Because literature too often is neglected in the classroom, the writer has long believed that we need a special literature period in the elementary school schedule. Such a provision at each level or at each age, regardless of traditional or innovative curriculum, would focus teacher attention on the necessity of including literature in her plans.

Let us point out that there are, however, two complications: the teacher's knowledge of literature and attitude toward reading. Generally, teachers at all levels have a limited knowledge of the literature available and almost no understanding of the critical appraisal of it. We grant that the number of juvenile books published each year makes keeping up with personal reading almost an impossible feat. Prices limit the number any one of us can purchase personally, although paperbacks afford a splendid savings. Yet we cannot guide children in what they read if we ourselves lack acquaintance with a great many books. The fact that a story has been printed does not mean that it possesses merit. A teacher must learn to judge what should have a place in the program.

Similarly, the teacher's own reaction to reading is of particular importance since we know that enthusiasm or lack of it is easily communicated. In a recent reading survey of female teachers, Roeder (6) found that a "lot of them do not read much and do not like to read." Reading was defined liberally as "had read or begun a book for her own enjoyment." Fifty percent of the teachers preferred other forms of leisure. Some frankly stated that they did not like to read because it was "too much work." Roeder speculated as to whether the teachers disliked reading because they themselves did not read well. Disturbed at his findings, Roeder suggested screening prospective teachers according to their "reading power" and having inservice programs for teachers. Surely, if teachers are not skilled readers and are negative toward reading, we must think of the implications for children and young people in their classrooms.

How, then, can we use literature to develop reading skills? Wilson (9) insists that a child who has learned basic techniques is a problem reader if he does not want to read. Nila Banton Smith (8) points out that, as a child becomes more proficient in using skills, the more he enjoys reading: "No teacher should use literature solely as a basis for teaching reading skills, but she certainly should use literature as a medium for applying skills in joyful, purposeful reading." Smith cautions that the literature must be within the readability level of the individual. Truly, any teacher can help a child acquire a broad, solid foundation in reading; gain both fluency and speed; and develop skills of interpretation and appreciation. We must be cautious, however, that we do not ruin the pleasure of the child by inefficient, excessive emphasis upon technique. Some technical understanding, however, does enhance appreciation of literature.

illustrations of skills

Some specific illustrations may clarify how literature may be used at various stages of maturity to develop some reading skills. There is an attempt here not to be all inclusive but merely suggestive. Three books for different developmental levels and, finally, poetry will serve as examples. The first book is *Hildilid's Night* (7), an honor book for the 1972 Caldecott Award. Hildilid was an old woman who lived up in the hills and who hated the night. If she could get rid of the night, she thought, sun would always shine on her house. She said: "I do not know why no one has thought of chasing away the night before." She attempted many means but, no matter what she did, the night was always there until sunrise. Finally, she turned her back on it and went to sleep. Hearing the story read aloud first, the small youngster will find a familiar idea that will bring pleasure and humor. What little child ever really wants to see night and bedtime come? The child can identify with the character of Hildilid, even though she may be considered a little foolish. The child has appreciation of the theme, but here also is the evident understanding that the outcome is inevitable; the night cannot be chased away. What fun children should have predicting that! What can Hildilid possibly do? It is so simple and droll; she turns her back and goes to sleep! The wording is particularly powerful for imagery:

> She swept and scrubbed and scoured and whisked,
> but whenever she looked out of her window,
> the night was still there,
> like dust behind rafters.

To cram the night into a sack she "wadded and padded and pushed and stuffed," and "she even sneaked up on the shadows." Putting the huge caldron over the fire, she "ladled it, stirred it, simmered it, bubbled it, tasted it, and burned it, but she could not boil away the night." What splendid words—"let's talk together about them, boys and girls"—they stimulate the imagination, even with Lobel's descriptive illustrations. How unobtrusively can literary tastes and interests be furthered. How easily can such reading skills be developed through this book!

At a more advanced level, though still for the primary age child, is Ness' *DoYouHaveTheTime, Lydia?* (5). Though the story may be read aloud or taped, a second and third grader will try to read it. Lydia, her younger brother, Andy, and her father lived on an "island in the middle of a warm and noisy sea." Every day her father was busy. Every day Lydia was so busy doing so much that she never finished anything. Andy didn't know how to do anything, and when he asked Lydia for help, she always told him she didn't have time. Her father would say, "If you *take* time you can *have* time." One morning Andy brought an old lobster trap to his sister and asked her to help him make a racing car for a race that afternoon; a dog would be the prize. Lydia promised to do so when she had time, and she did make a start. But when she looked for a steering wheel, her attention was distracted by too many other things. The dog was given to someone else, and

Literature Develops Reading Skills

Andy, in tears, fled from Lydia. Lydia took time to cry, and then she persuaded Andy that the car was a fire engine. Promising him a ladder for it, she was learning that if she *took* time she could *have* time. Bright, sunny pictures illuminate the story.

Here, again, any child with an older brother or sister can relive the experience of Andy. The child can judge the title of the book and note how the words are run together, grasp the details and follow the story events, sense the emotions of Andy and Lydia, decide Lydia's character at first and then later, and discover the satisfaction of the ending. Drawing inferences from the language of taking time and having time is also critical reading which will challenge good thinking. These skills of interpretation and appreciation are founded upon the basic skills of learning to read.

For intermediate grades, Burch's *Queenie Peavy* (1) is a fine book. The story starts with a surefire attention-getter; the first two lines read, ''Queenie Peavy was the only girl in Cotton Junction who could chew tobacco. She could also spit it—and with deadly aim.'' (What kind of a character is Queenie? Evaluate her actions now and later in the book. Has the author given proof at the very beginning of his facility with words? Can you visualize Queenie?) Because of her accuracy at throwing rocks, Queenie runs into trouble and is blamed for something which she did not do. Her mother works long hours at a factory for a wage too low to keep them in comfort. Children taunt Queenie about her father's being in prison. Idolizing her father, she knows that things will be perfect when he is paroled. Instead, he is returned to prison. Queenie battles her own emotions in a struggle to think before acting, and she starts trying to accept life as it is rather than as she wishes it to be.

Comprehension, word analysis, phonics, and organizational skills are the foundation for many other skills: comparing the characters of the mother and father, deciding the action had you been Queenie, finding the central idea of a chapter and of the book, recognizing Queenie's growth, determining the significance of an event, finding the factual background of the story, feeling like Queenie, trying to understand realities in many lives, exploring poverty and pathos, grasping cause-effect relationships of Queenie's behavior, deciding on the story atmosphere, and knowing the author's purpose. These and other skills in reading literature can be the focus of discussion which can enrich the life of the reader.

Finally, poetry offers its own contribution to reading skills. Probably nowhere else are there such special words for the purpose which the poet has in mind, as Carl Sandburg once stated. How are words used to illuminate the commonplace, to give imagery, to carry connotation, to evoke emotion, to provide color, and to give that singing quality that led Vachel Lindsay to call poetry a song art? What makes poetry poetry instead of prose? What are the surface meanings? Are there levels to deeper meanings? Why is figurative language important? Let teacher and children talk and delve into these ideas. Let them check poetic form, language, and technique. Steer clear of too much of the analysis, meter, and memorization so common to high school and college. Work for enjoyment and sensitivity of insight. Then, as the teacher reads aloud, let the voice signal meaning, emotion, and emphasis. Choral speaking is a splendid device for poetry rendition. When children learn to read poetry and divide it for verse choirs, comprehension must be present as well as appreciation.

Overheard on a Saltmarsh (4)

Nymph, nymph, what are your beads?

Green glass, goblin. Why do you stare at them?

Give them me.
No.

Give them me. Give them me.
No.

Then I will howl all night in the reeds,
Lie in the mud and howl for them.

Goblin, why do you love them so?

They are better than stars or water,
Better than voices of winds that sing,
Better than any man's fair daughter,
Your green glass beads on a silver ring.

Hush, I stole them out of the moon.

Give me your beads, I desire them.
No.

I will howl in a deep lagoon
For your green glass beads, I love them so.
Give them me. Give them.
No.

—Harold Monro

The sound of words; the conversation of two beings; the voice as interpreter—all this is poetry!

Literature Develops Reading Skills

summary

In summary, the common skills of beginning reading may be reinforced in the rich area of literature. They may expand and mature and may become closely allied to new skills such as developing sensitivity in interpretation, critical thinking, and appreciation. When a child achieves this state, reading and literature will be one.

references

1. Burch, Robert. *Queenie Peavy.* New York: Viking, 1966.
2. Gag, Wanda. *Millions of Cats.* New York: Coward-McCann, 1928.
3. Goodman, Kenneth. "Reading: The Key is in Children's Language," *Reading Teacher,* 25 (March 1972), 505-508.
4. Monro, Harold. "Overheard on a Saltmarsh," *Children of Love.* London: Poetry Book Shop, 1913.
5. Ness, Evaline. *DoYouHaveTheTime, Lydia?* New York: Dutton, 1971.
6. "Of Preaching and Practicing," *Concern* (AACTE Newsletter), 2 (November 1971), 6.
7. Ryan, Cheli. *Hildilid's Night.* New York: Macmillan, 1971.
8. Smith, Nila Banton. *Reading Instruction for Today's Children.* Englewood Cliffs, New Jersey: Prentice-Hall, 1963, 394.
9. Wilson, Robert M. *Diagnostic and Remedial Reading for Classroom and Clinic* (2nd ed.). Columbus, Ohio: Merrill, 1972, 2-3.

This paper presents an adaptation of the Hilda Taba strategies as a method for teaching critical reading skills. Sample lessons are included.

utilizing social studies content to develop critical reading

ruth g. mueller
case western reserve university

Elementary school educators have generally included the skill of critical reading as an important objective in the curriculum. Many professional reading texts list critical reading as a comprehension skill, most often the last one to be named. This position is indicative of the place that critical reading usually occupies in elementary schools.

Evidence indicates that little or no time is spent on critical reading instruction in grades one through six. Explanations for the lack of critical reading instruction in many schools are listed in *The First R* as: 1) instruction at the college level which does not give adequate training for implementing the instruction, 2) lack of teacher education in logical thinking skills, 3) little aid in most basal reader teaching guides, 4) classroom reading instruction which stresses readiness and guided reading, and 5) testing pupils primarily for literal comprehension (1).

The dual purpose of this paper is 1) to develop a rationale for critical reading skills in the form of a coherent framework and 2) to present a strategy for critical reading instruction which is logically consistent with the nature of the skill. The central hypotheses are that there are certain cognitive skills which are basic to and prerequisite for the development of critical reading ability and that these skills can be increased by instruction.

critical reading

Since critical reading is generally considered to be a subskill of the reading process, examination of the nature of critical reading should first consider the nature of reading. Definitions of reading range from the description of the process of decoding printed symbols for meaning to the more general statement that reading is thinking. Components of the reading process are given various terms, but generally included are the skills of word perception, comprehension, reaction and assimilation (*10*). The processes of reaction and assimilation are considered basic to critical reading. According to many definitions, critical reading is the ability to analyze what is read and make logical evaluations. The definition probably most often quoted is Robinson's, which states that critical reading is the "judgment of the veracity, validity, or worth of what is read, based on sound criteria or standards developed through previous experience" (*7*).

Further consideration of the nature of critical reading can include an examination of the mental operations which may be used in the process. Many educators believe critical reading utilizes operations similar to critical thinking. Among these, Russell (*9*) and Glaser (*5*) state that critical reading utilizes critical thinking skills in the evaluation of what is read. Acceptance of this assumption implies that cognitive operations as they relate to critical thinking may be considered as part of the nature of critical reading.

The feasibility of critical reading instruction at the elementary level is considered in the following section.

critical reading at the elementary level

Much of the critical reading instruction in the schools is at the secondary level. Support for this observation is attained indirectly by Buros' *Reading Tests and Reviews* (*2*) which lists critical reading tests for college and secondary school levels only. One of the tests listed was developed by Glaser (*5*) in a study which is considered by many to be a landmark in critical reading research. In addition to the evaluating instrument, Glaser developed teaching strategies and a rationale of critical reading that is frequently referred to in the literature. For some time following this study, research on critical reading was concentrated at the secondary level. Explanations for this concentration of attention may lie in the hierarchical concept of reading skills as espoused by educators such as Robinson (*7*) and Russell (*9*). This concept places critical reading at the highest level of the continuum of complexity. Also, as Taba (12) reports, a widely accepted assumption is that thinking cannot take place until a sufficient body of knowledge is accumulated, in order to have something to "think with." The fallacy of this assumption can be demonstrated by the studies of Taba (11), Ennis (4), and Wolf (13). In addition, Russell states that no "age of reason" stage of mental development is requisite to developing critical reading abilities. Instead, a gradual increase in the complexity of the situations, which are the basis of instruction, is what should be considered. The degree of success attained by Wolf, Taba, Ennis, and others, along with the need for such instruction as reported in *The First R,* suggests that the improvement in critical reading abilities of young children is both feasible and desirable.

Based on the assumption that critical reading uses cognitive skills to process the material read, cognitive skill instruction at the elementary level is investigated in the following section.

teaching cognitive skills

Though intellectual development of pupils is accepted by schools as an educational objective, specific instruction with identified cognitive objectives is rare. The influence of instruction on the level of cognitive operation by pupils is demonstrated by studies which indicate that the cognitive level of teachers' questions determines the cognitive level of response by pupils (11).

Five studies of teaching have centered on cognitive objectives of teaching. Studies by Davis and Tinsley (3) and Rogers (8) analyzed teachers' questions which were recorded using a standard observation record. Recall questions were employed most of the time by the teachers. In addition, Rogers found that the inservice program aimed at varying the cognitive level of teachers' questions did not significantly alter patterns of teaching.

Hiparm (6) conducted a study to explore instruction in logic as a means of increasing the critical thinking ability of pupils. Because his study was limited in scope by the small number of subjects and was restricted to the upper-level intelligence range, his positive results are not widely generalizable. His study is an example, however, of the growing number of researchers who are dissatisfied with the results of the large number of studies which have attempted to improve critical thinking skills of children by instruction in methods of problem solving and scientific inquiry.

Results of Wolf's study (13) would tend to support Hiparm's contention that instruction in logic can help develop pupils' skills at logical reasoning as a component of critical reading. At all grade levels of the study, grades one through six, the experimental classes showed significantly higher scores on the criterion measure, with the greatest gains occurring in the measure of logical reasoning.

According to Taba (*12*) acquisition of the cognitive skills of critical reading requires the use of a teaching strategy considerably different from those commonly used. Teachers have traditionally considered themselves transmitters of information, and to allow a child enough freedom to learn to reach his own decision or interpretation requires less telling and more stimulating of a learner's thinking. While information can be learned through listening or reading, active mental processes such as these cognitive skills described by Taba cannot be learned by following the thought processes of either a book or a teacher, unless a learner also has the opportunity to internalize and build on the cognitive skills through use. Some of the ways in which this concept of teaching may be implemented are presented in the following section.

critical reading instruction

Taba (*12*) has attempted to identify some of the cognitive tasks, some of the skills that may contribute to these tasks, and some instructional strategies for developing these cognitive task objectives. The major cognitive tasks she describes are concept formation, data interpretation, and concept application.

As proposed by Taba, cognitive skills are developed sequentially from concrete operations to more complex and abstract processes. In her framework she arranges these skills in a hierarchical order and identifies the covert and overt mental processes related to each skill.

The most concrete level, concept formation, includes the activities of enumeration and listing, grouping, categorizing, labeling and subsuming. Interpretation of data, the second level of cognitive tasks, is composed of identifying points, explaining items of information, and making inferences based on the data supplied. The most abstract level is the application of principles, which includes the prediction of consequences, explaining unfamiliar data, and explaining and supporting hypotheses.

Because Taba's framework provides a relationship between overt activities and cognitive skills which have been identified as aspects of critical reading, it provides a basis for planning an organized instructional program for developing the cognitive skills of critical reading.

The first two cognitive tasks, concept formation and interpretation of data, are used in this paper as the basis for planning critical reading instruction. In the study directed by Taba (11) in which she developed this framework, social studies was chosen as the area for content instruction. This paper also presents social studies as the instructional content.

Using the conceptual framework for cognitive skill development presented by Taba, together with those reading skills which are concerned with eliciting the basic data presented in the reading material, the objectives of this program are the ability to: 1) state or infer the author's purpose, 2) identify or state the main idea of a passage and supporting details, 3) detect the organization of the information presented, 4) determine the author's intended meaning of words through context, 5) differentiate between statements of fact and opinion, 6) enumerate and categorize items of information, 7) explain identified information, 8) propose inferences, and 9) reach and support conclusions or generalizations.

The strategies used to reach these objectives fall into two categories: the use of organized materials and semicontrolled discussions (12). The level of the materials is appropriate for fifth grade.

The use of organized materials is designed to teach pupils the skills of comprehension which are included in the first seven objectives stated above. The opportunity to develop the abilities described in the remaining two objectives is provided through the discussions.

The teaching strategy used with organized materials is the use of a retrieval chart (12). By using a chart to organize the information presented in a passage, relationships are evident, missing information becomes obvious, and teachers can more easily accomplish comparisons of characteristics or phenomena. It is suggested that, after pupils have read the passage, the outline of the chart be presented and the pupils and teacher together supply the information for the appropriate categories. The passage in Example 1 describes a training program for young Spartans. While cause and effect relationships are not stated, the information is presented as such. The passage has no title in order to require the reader to rely on the information in the passage to determine the main idea or the author's purpose.

The retrieval chart may be used in different ways. For younger children, the teacher may want to have the pupils identify items of information in a passage and have these listed on the chalkboard. Then these items may be transferred to the appropriate categories on the chart, with the pupils participating in this process. With older students, the teacher may go directly to the completion of the retrieval chart. The category labels should represent the type of information presented and/or major concepts considered in the discussion. The presentation of the information in retrieval chart form is found in Example 2.

Such a discussion-teaching technique allows the teacher to pose questions that will develop the student's ability to see the cause and effect relationship, to infer the result of the conduct, and to control techniques used. The discussion is semicontrolled because the information in the passage and the teacher's questions give direction for the discussion and because the discussion is used to reach specific cognitive objectives. The content of the answers is not determined by the questions, but the level of thinking is influenced by the types of questions. A suggested guide for discussion is presented in Example 3. An additional sample lesson appears in Examples 4, 5, and 6.

lesson 1: example 1

Sparta had a well-planned training program for children. The purpose was to raise citizens who would be strong and obedient so that the state would be able to defend itself against invaders.

Young Spartans were trained to be able to withstand discomfort. One part of their training was to wear the same kind of garment all year which helped them withstand weather changes from hot to cold.

Food was also used to train the children to live without the usual comforts. They were not allowed to continue to eat until they were full. They were given enough food to keep healthy, but they were not accustomed to eating fancy foods and big meals. As a result, they were able to exist on little food during long marches.

To make sure that no boy would lack someone to watch over him, any citizen was allowed to punish a boy for any wrong he might do. The boys were taught to keep their hands inside their cloaks, to walk in silence, and to keep their heads down with their eyes on the ground.

It would have been hard to find a healthier or stronger person than the Spartan citizen.

Author's conclusion:
Spartans were strong and healthy.
Cognitive objectives:
identifying and enumerating items of information,
grouping,
categorizing,
detecting organization of material presented, and
detecting missing information.

retrieval chart: example 2

	Practice	Result
Clothing	Wear same garment all year.	Able to stand weather changes without adjusting clothing.
Food	Not allowed to eat until full. No fancy foods or big meals.	Able to go without much food on long marches.
Conduct and Control	Any citizen could punish a boy. Boys were taught to: keep hands inside cloaks, walk in silence, keep heads down, keep eyes on ground.	Many adults available to supervise boys. (Intended result?)

discussion guide: example 3

Objectives and suggested questions.
1. To state the main idea.

    What does the author talk about most? Does the author tell why Spartans wanted to treat boys that way? Which sentence gives a name to the treatment for boys?
2. To state author's intention.

    Does he state it? What did we say he talked about most? Was he saying that this is a desirable way to treat boys? Why do you think he wrote the article?
3. To determine cause and effect relationship.

    What did they think would happen because the boys didn't eat much? Why did they wear the same type of clothing all year? What else might happen? Same types of questions may be asked for the other practices. Do you think that the results they wanted always occurred? Why or why not?
4. To make inferences.

    Why do you think that they made boys walk like they did? How well do you think boys behaved when any adult could punish them? Can we decide what might be a possible result of this aspect of training?

5. To make generalizations, go beyond information given.
   Do you think the Spartans treated boys badly? Why or why not? How are you treated by your parents as compared to the Spartan boys? Do you think you're as healthy as they were? Why or why not? What other ways can people improve their health?

lesson 2: example 4

A name almost forgotten during the period following the Supreme Court ruling against segregation is that of Mrs. Rose Parks of Montgomery, Alabama. Mrs. Parks did a very simple thing: She refused to get up and give her seat on the bus to a white man. She was tired, and she was fed up. "It just happened," she explained later, "that the driver made a demand and I just didn't feel like obeying it."

This is the way that the Montgomery bus boycott of 1955 and 1956 began. For 381 days Negroes refused to ride Montgomery buses and the boycott ended only after the Supreme Court ruled that bus segregation was illegal.

But the boycott had another effect in influencing what was to happen later. Mrs. Parks' refusal to give up her bus seat was an act of nonviolent resistance. Nonviolent resistance is a peaceful means by which citizens can protest about conditions which they believe are unjust. The boycott was the first nonviolent action by a large group of people that was intended to break down segregation. The success of the Montgomery boycott showed that protesting against an unjust law by peaceful means can help end unfairness. Most important, it showed that black Americans realized that court decisions were not enough and that something more was needed to end the segregation system.

retrieval chart: example 5

	Action	Reason for action	Result
Individual	Refused to give bus seat to white man.	Didn't feel like obeying driver's demand.	Bus boycott began, boycott showed that peaceful protests can be successful.
Groups	Supreme Court ruling.		Segregation on buses illegal.

Author's conclusion:

The success of the bus boycott showed that peaceful protests can help end unfairness and that black Americans realized that more than court decisions were needed to end segregation.

discussion guide: example 6

Objectives and suggested questions.

1. To state the main idea:

    Is the main idea stated? What was the reason for the boycott? What did the author say started the boycott? Why do you think the author wanted to tell this story?

2. To state the author's intention.

    Does the author state his reason for writing the story? Does he give facts only, or does he include his own opinions? Are the last two sentences facts or conclusions reached by the author? Do you think this passage was written to express the author's own point of view? Why or why not?

3. To determine cause and effect relationship and make inferences.

    What happened when Mrs. Parks decided not to give up her seat? After the boycott was started, what happened? Does a boycott usually include a few people or many? Why do you think the Supreme Court decided to end the boycott and the bus segregation? Why did all of these events happen?

4. To make inferences and go beyond information given.

    Do you think that bus segregation was a law? Why or why not? What do you think might have happened to Mrs. Parks after that day? Why? In the last paragraph, the author gives a second result of the boycott. What action caused all of these things to happen, according to the author? What else might have happened after the bus boycott?

The strategies presented in the examples can be used and adapted for many varieties of content and for other grade levels. The use of structured lessons and discussions provides the opportunity for reaching specific cognitive skill objectives, for allowing pupils to reach their own decisions, for building cognitive skills through use, and for developing proficiency in critical reading skills.

references

1. Austin, M., and C. Morrison. *The First R.* New York: Macmillan, 1963.
2. Buros, O. *Reading Tests and Reviews.* New York: Gryphon Press, 1968.

Developing Critical Reading

3. Davis, O., Jr., and D. Tinsley. "Cognitive Objectives Revealed by Classroom Questions Asked by Social Studies Student Teachers," *Peabody Journal of Education,* 45 (1967).

4. Ennis, R. *Critical Thinking Readiness in Grades 1-12,* report of Cooperative Research Project #1680. Ithaca, New York: Cornell University, 1962.

5. Glaser, E. *An Experiment in the Development of Critical Thinking,* Contributions to Education No. 842. New York: Teachers College, Columbia University, 1941.

6. Hiparm, G. "An Experiment in Developing Critical Thinking in Children," *Journal of Experimental Education,* 26 (1967).

7. Robinson, H. M. "Developing Critical Reading," Proceedings of the Annual Education and Reading Conference, 11. Newark, Delaware: University of Delaware, 1964.

8. Rogers, V. "Varying the Cognitive Levels of Classroom Questions in Elementary Social Studies: An Analysis of the Use of Questions by Student Teachers," unpublished doctoral dissertation, University of Texas at Austin, 1969.

9. Russell, D. *Children's Thinking.* Waltham, Massachusetts: Blaisdell, 1956.

10. Simmons, J. "Reasoning Through Reading," *Journal of Reading,* 3 (1962), 311-314.

11. Taba, H. *Teaching Strategies and Cognitive Functioning in Elementary School Children,* USOE Cooperative Research Project No. 2404, San Francisco State College, 1966.

12. Taba, H. "Implementing Thinking as an Objective in Social Studies," *Effective Thinking in the Social Studies,* Thirty-Seventh Yearbook of National Council for the Social Studies, 1967, 25-50.

13. Wolf, W., et al. *Critical Reading Ability of Elementary School Children.* Columbus, Ohio: Ohio State University Research Foundation, 1967.